STÉPHANE MALLARMÉ

SELECTED POETRY AND PROSE

STÉPHANE MALLARMÉ

SELECTED POETRY AND PROSE

Edited by Mary Ann Caws

A NEW DIRECTIONS BOOK

ACKNOWLEDGMENTS
Grateful acknowledgment is given to *Landrona, The Paris Review,* and *Yale French Studies,* where the translations by Cid Corman, Paul Auster, and James Lawler included here first appeared.
The following are reprinted by permission of their original publishers: translation by Barbara Johnson from Jacques Derrida, *Dissemination,* translated by Barbara Johnson (Copyright © 1981 by Barbara Johnson) by permission of Chicago University Press; translations by Patricia Terry and Maurice Z. Shroder (Copyright © 1975 by Patricia Terry and Maurice Z. Shroder) from *Modern French Poetry: A Bilingual Anthology,* edited by Patricia Terry and Serge Garronsky, by permission of Columbia University Press; translation by Brian Coffey (Copyright © 1965 by Brian Coffey) by permission of the Dolmen Press, Dublin; translation by Frederick Morgan (Copyright © 1958 by Frederick Morgan) from the *Anchor Book of French Poetry,* by permission of Frederick Morgan; translations by Bradford Cook (Copyright © 1956 by The Johns Hopkins University Press) from *Selected Poems, Essays, and Letters* of Stéphane Mallarmé, edited by Bradford Cook; translations by Roger Fry (Copyright 1951 by New Directions) by permission of Chatto & Windus, Ltd.; translations by Hubert Creekmore (Copyright 1942 by The Modern Poetry Association) by permission of the Editor of *Poetry;* excerpt from *Mallarmé's Igitur* by Robert Greer Cohn (Copyright © 1981 by Robert Greer Cohn) by permission of University of California Press.

Library of Congress Cataloging in Publication Data

Mallarmé, Stéphane, 1842-1898.
    Selected poetry and prose.
    (A New Directions Book)
    I. Caws, Mary Ann. II. Title.
PQ2344.A2   1982b   841'.8   81-18899
ISBN 0-8112-0822-2   AACR2
ISBN 0-8112-0823-0 (pbk.)

Manufactured in the United States of America
New Directions Books are printed on acid-free paper
First published clothbound as a New Directions Paperbook 529 in 1982
Published simultaneously in Canada by Penguin Books Canada Ltd.

New Directions Books are published for James Laughlin
by New Directions Publishing Corporation
80 Eighth Avenue, New York 10011
FIFTH PRINTING

Contents

Quant au livre/As for the Book

THE TRANSLATORS

PAUL AUSTER

MARY ANN CAWS

PETER CAWS

BRIAN COFFEY

BRADFORD COOK

CID CORMAN

HUBERT CREEKMORE

ROGER FRY

BARBARA JOHNSON

JAMES LAWLER

GEORGE MOORE

FREDERICK MORGAN

MAURICE Z. SHRODER

PATRICIA TERRY

MARC WIDERSHIEN

Editor's Preface

"some gesture vehement and lost"
—Stéphane Mallarmé, "Action Restricted"

Selection is already a gesture, and an homage. It is to be hoped that the positive side of this gesture will outweigh its foolhardy nature: to publish any Mallarmé in translation is dangerous, as anyone will agree. There is no possible (and readable) way of conveying each of the multiple meanings of the intricately styled verse or the equally intricate (and often more obscure) prose while keeping the forms Mallarmé chose. On the other hand, to sacrifice the forms is often inadvisable, since for Mallarmé the complexities of poetic form alone compensate for the inevitable imperfection of language. Footnotes explaining even some of the senses, kept or lost, implicit or explicit, would weigh too heavily upon the translated text, for the original is seldom unambiguous and rarely heavy.

Mallarmé's diversity is probably best served by diverse hands: thus the variety of translators, over a dozen, from the beginning of the century to our contemporaries. I have chosen what seem to me the best versions from a double point of view: exactitude, formal and meaningful, and poetry (a quality both of verse and prose). Some of the renderings have been previously published, while others were undertaken specifically for this volume. Included here are most of the major poems, selections from the letters, essays, and prose poems, and the play-narration *Igitur* as well as the celebrated visual poem *Un Coup de dés*.

The language is not familiar: Mallarmé would have condemned that roundly. He preferred obliqueness, cherished distance in his work—compelled his reader to sense its foreignness. These translations, from those of the Symbolists and Bloomsbury (George Moore and Roger Fry) to those done expressly for this project, have tried to accept that sense, while also making their own. I should like to thank, in particular, for their advice, Robert Greer Cohn, James Laughlin, Patricia Terry, and Micheline Tison–Braun.

This selection can be best described by Mallarmé's title for one of his major essays, included here. The "Action Restricted" is at once a major undertaking and a restricted one, voluntarily assumed, in which the vehemence particular to the gesture referred to in the epigraph may be exercised with no worry as to the outcome or the utility. Perhaps, like some Mallarméan lace, self-abolishing and yet not completely effaced, the gesture will not be wholly lost. These readings, individually and collectively, add on to others gone before them:

> *and this*
> *maybe not*
> *too late*
> *tribute to*
> *once Stéphane Mallarmé*
> —Louis Zukofsky, "A"

Mary Ann Caws

STÉPHANE MALLARMÉ

SELECTED POETRY AND PROSE

SALUT

Rien, cette écume, vierge vers
A ne désigner que la coupe;
Telle loin se noie une troupe
De sirènes mainte à l'envers.

Nous naviguons, ô mes divers
Amis, moi déjà sur la poupe
Vous l'avant fastueux qui coupe
Le flot de foudres et d'hivers;

Une ivresse belle m'engage
Sans craindre même son tangage
De porter debout ce salut

Solitude, récif, étoile
A n'importe ce qui valut
Le blanc souci de notre toile.

SALUTE

Nothing, this spume, virgin verse
Only to point to the cup;
So afar many a troupe
Of sirens drowns in reverse.

We navigate, O my diverse
Friends, me now on the poop
You the sumptuous prow to reap
Lightnings and seasons perverse;

A fine ivresse brings me
Fearless of its very pitch
To bear upright this salute

Solitude, reef, star
To whatever is worth
The white concern of our sheet.

CID CORMAN

Premiers poèmes

APPARITION

La lune s'attristait. Des séraphins en pleurs
Rêvant, l'archet aux doigts, dans le calme des fleurs
Vaporeuses, tiraient de mourantes violes
De blancs sanglots glissant sur l'azur des corolles.
—C'était le jour béni de ton premier baiser.
Ma songerie aimant à me martyriser
S'enivrait savamment du parfum de tristesse
Que même sans regret et sans déboire laisse
La cueillaison d'un Rêve au cœur qui l'a cueilli.
J'errais donc, l'œil rivé sur le pavé vieilli
Quand avec du soleil aux cheveux, dans la rue
Et dans le soir, tu m'es en riant apparue
Et j'ai cru voir la fée au chapeau de clarté
Qui jadis sur mes beaux sommeils d'enfant gâté
Passait, laissant toujours de ses mains mal fermées
Neiger de blancs bouquets d'étoiles parfumées.

LE PITRE CHÂTIÉ

Yeux, lacs avec ma simple ivresse de renaître
Autre que l'histrion qui du geste évoquais
Comme plume la suie ignoble des quinquets,
J'ai troué dans le mur de toile une fenêtre.

De ma jambe et des bras limpide nageur traître,
A bonds multipliés, reniant le mauvais
Hamlet! c'est comme si dans l'onde j'innovais
Mille sépulcres pour y vierge disparaître.

First Poems

APPARITION

The moon was saddening. Seraphim in tears
Dreaming, bow in hand, in the calm of vaporous
Flowers, were drawing from dying violins
White sobs gliding down blue corollas
—It was the blessed day of your first kiss.
My dreaming loving to torment me
Was drinking deep of the perfume of sadness
That even without regret and deception is left
By the gathering of a Dream in the heart which has gathered it.
I wandered then, my eyes on the worn pavement
When with the sun in your hair, and in the street
In the evening, you in laughter appeared to me
And I thought I saw the fairy with her cap of brightness
Who once on the beauty-sleeps of my spoilt childhood
Passed, letting always her half-closed hands
Snow down white bouquets of perfumed stars.

ROGER FRY

THE CLOWN CHASTISED

Eyes, lakes with my simple passion to be reborn
Other than the actor, evoking with gestures
For feather the ugly soot of stage lights,
I have pierced a window in the canvas wall.

Clear traitor swimmer, with my legs and arms
Leaping and bounding, denying the wrong
Hamlet! as if I created in the wave
A thousand tombs in which to virgin disappear.

5

Hilare or de cymbale à des poings irrité,
Tout à coup le soleil frappe la nudité
Qui pure s'exhala de ma fraîcheur de nacre,

Rance nuit de la peau quand sur moi vous passiez,
Ne sachant pas, ingrat! que c'était tout mon sacre,
Ce fard noyé dans l'eau perfide des glaciers.

Joyous gold of the cymbal fists have inflamed,
Suddenly the sun strikes the barrenness pure
Exhaled from my coolness like mother-of-pearl.

Stale night of the skin when you swept over me,
Ungrateful! Ignorant of my whole consecration,
That grease paint drowned in faithless glacier water.

MARY ANN CAWS

Du Parnasse contemporain

LES FENÊTRES

Las du triste hôpital, et de l'encens fétide
Qui monte en la blancheur banale des rideaux
Vers le grand crucifix ennuyé du mur vide,
Le moribond sournois y redresse un vieux dos,

Se traîne et va, moins pour chauffer sa pourriture
Que pour voir du soleil sur les pierres, coller
Les poils blancs et les os de la maigre figure
Aux fenêtres qu'un beau rayon clair veut hâler.

Et la bouche, fiévreuse et d'azur bleu vorace,
Telle, jeune, elle alla respirer son trésor,
Une peau virginale et de jadis! encrasse
D'un long baiser amer les tièdes carreaux d'or.

Ivre, il vit, oubliant l'horreur des saintes huiles,
Les tisanes, l'horloge et le lit infligé,
La toux; et quand le soir saigne parmi les tuiles,
Son œil, à l'horizon de lumière gorgé,

Voit des galères d'or, belles comme des cygnes,
Sur un fleuve de pourpre et de parfums dormir
En berçant l'éclair fauve et riche de leurs lignes
Dans un grand nonchaloir chargé de souvenir!

Ainsi, pris du dégoût de l'homme à l'âme dure
Vautré dans le bonheur, où ses seuls appétits
Mangent, et qui s'entête à chercher cette ordure
Pour l'offrir à la femme allaitant ses petits,

From Contemporary Parnassus

THE WINDOWS

Tired of the sad hospital and fetid incense
Arising like the banal whiteness of veils
To the great bored crucifix on the empty wall,
The crafty dying man his back sets straight,

Then drags along and, less to warm his decay
Than see the sunshine on the stones, will press
His white hair and the bones of his gaunt face
On the windows that a fine clear sunbeam burns;

And fevered, greedy for deep azure, the mouth,
As, youthful, it would breathe its wealth away,
A virgin skin of long ago! befouls
With a long, bitter kiss the warm golden panes.

And drunk, he lives, the horror of holy oils
Forgot, and cordials and clocks, the bed prescribed,
The cough; and when evening bleeds along the tiles,
His gaze, gorged on the horizon of light,

Sees golden galleys, beautiful as swans,
On a ruddy, perfumed river, cradling to sleep
The tawny, rich light of their echelons
In vast nonchalance charged with memories!

So, filled with disgust for the man whose soul is callous,
Sprawled in comforts where his hungering
Is fed, stubborn in searching out this ordure
To offer the wife who nurses his offspring,

Je fuis et je m'accroche à toutes les croisées
D'où l'on tourne l'épaule à la vie, et, béni,
Dans leur verre, lavé d'éternelles rosées,
Que dore le matin chaste de l'Infini

Je me mire et me vois ange! et je meurs, et j'aime
—Que la vitre soit l'art, soit la mysticité—
A renaître, portant mon rêve en diadème,
Au ciel antérieur où fleurit la Beauté!

Mais, hélas! Ici-bas est maître : sa hantise
Vient m'écœurer parfois jusqu'en cet abri sûr,
Et le vomissement impur de la Bêtise
Me force à me boucher le nez devant l'azur.

Est-il moyen, ô Moi qui connais l'amertume,
D'enfoncer le cristal par le monstre insulté
Et de m'enfuir, avec mes deux ailes sans plume
—Au risque de tomber pendant l'éternité?

ANGOISSE

Je ne viens pas ce soir vaincre ton corps, ô bête
En qui vont les péchés d'un peuple, ni creuser
Dans tes cheveux impurs une triste tempête
Sous l'incurable ennui que verse mon baiser:

Je demande à ton lit le lourd sommeil sans songes
Planant sous les rideaux inconnus du remords,
Et que tu peux goûter après tes noirs mensonges,
Toi qui sur le néant en sais plus que les morts.

Car le Vice, rongeant ma native noblesse
M'a comme toi marqué de sa stérilité,
Mais tandis que ton sein de pierre est habité

I flee and cling to all the window frames
Whence one can turn his back on life in scorn,
And, blest, in their glass, by eternal dewdrops laved
And gilded by the Infinite's chaste morn,

I peer and see myself an angel! I die, I long
—Let the window be art, be mystic state—
To be reborn, wearing my dream as a crown,
In the previous heaven where Beauty flowered great!

But oh! the World Below is lord: its spell
Still nauseates me in this safe retreat,
And the reeking spew of Stupidity compels
Me to hold my nose before the azure sheet.

Is this a way, oh Self who knows gall stings,
To burst the crystal stupidity vilifies,
And take flight, on my two unfeathered wings
—At the risk of falling through eternal skies?

HUBERT CREEKMORE

ANGUISH

I do not come to make your flesh less proud tonight, O beast
In whom the sins of a race take root, nor to stir up
In the hive of your hair a sorrowful storm
By the incurable ennui which my kiss pours out:

I ask of your bed the heavy dreamless sleep
Hovering under the drapes innocent of regret,
And which you after your black lies can taste
You who in your nothingness know more than the dead.

For the Vice, gnawing at my sensibilities
Has branded me like you with its sterility,
But whereas your breast of stone hides

Par un cœur que la dent d'aucun crime ne blesse,
Je fuis, pâle, défait, hanté par mon linceul,
Ayant peur de mourir lorsque je couche seul.

"LAS DE L'AMER REPOS
OÙ MA PARESSE OFFENSE . . ."

Las de l'amer repos où ma paresse offense
Une gloire pour qui jadis j'ai fui l'enfance
Adorable des bois de roses sous l'azur
Naturel, et plus las sept fois du pacte dur
De creuser par veillée une fosse nouvelle
Dans le terrain avare et froid de ma cervelle,
Fossoyeur sans pitié pour la stérilité,
—Que dire à cette Aurore, ô Rêves, visité
Par les roses, quand, peur de ses roses livides,
Le vaste cimetière unira les trous vides?—

Je veux délaisser l'Art vorace d'un pays
Cruel, et, souriant aux reproches vieillis
Que me font mes amis, le passé, le génie,
Et ma lampe qui sait pourtant mon agonie,
Imiter le Chinois au cœur limpide et fin
De qui l'extase pure est de peindre la fin
Sur ses tasses de neige à la lune ravie
D'une bizarre fleur qui parfume sa vie
Transparente, la fleur qu'il a sentie, enfant,
Au filigrane bleu de l'âme se greffant.
Et, la mort telle avec le seul rêve du sage,
Serein, je vais choisir un jeune paysage
Que je peindrais encor sur les tasses, distrait.
Une ligne d'azur mince et pâle serait
Un lac, parmi le ciel de porcelaine nue,
Un clair croissant perdu par une blanche nue

A heart which the tooth of no crime can pierce,
I flee, pale, exhausted, haunted by my shroud,
Fearing death while I lie alone.

MARC WIDERSHIEN

"WEARY OF BITTER EASE IN WHICH MY INDOLENCE . . ."

Weary of bitter ease in which my indolence
Offends a glory for which I fled the charm long since
Of childhood rose-embowered under natural arch
Of blue, and wearier sevenfold of this my harsh
Compact to dig each night a furrow once again
Into the cold and stingy soil of my brain,
Gravedigger with no pity for sterility,
—What can I tell this Dawn, by roses companied,
O Dreams, when out of terror for its ashen rose
The vast graveyard will merge these empty holes?

I would forsake the ravenous Art of cruel lands
And with a smile for all the age-old reprimands
Delivered by my friends and genius and the past
And by my lamp which knows my agony at last,
Would imitate the Chinese of limpid, delicate bent,
Whose purest ecstasy is but to paint the end
Upon his cups of snow new ravished from the moon
Of some exotic flower that constantly perfumed
His life, transparent flower he smelled in infancy,
Grafting itself upon the soul's blue filigree.
And like to death within the sage's only dream,
Serene, I'll choose a landscape young and evergreen
Which I also will paint on cups, preoccupied.
A line of azure, thin and pale, will signify
A lake, amid a sky of naked porcelain;
A shining crescent lost behind a white cloudscape

Trempe sa corne calme en la glace des eaux,
Non loin de trois grands cils d'émeraude, roseaux.

L'AZUR

De l'éternel azur la sereine ironie
Accable, belle indolemment comme les fleurs,
Le poëte impuissant qui maudit son génie
A travers un désert stérile de Douleurs.

Fuyant, les yeux fermés, je le sens qui regarde
Avec l'intensité d'un remords atterrant,
Mon âme vide. Où fuir? Et quelle nuit hagarde
Jeter, lambeaux, jeter sur ce mépris navrant?

Brouillards, montez! Versez vos cendres monotones
Avec de longs haillons de brume dans les cieux
Qui noiera le marais livide des automnes
Et bâtissez un grand plafond silencieux!

Et toi, sors des étangs léthéens et ramasse
En t'en venant la vase et les pâles roseaux,
Cher Ennui, pour boucher d'une main jamais lasse
Les grands trous bleus que font méchamment les oiseaux.

Encor! que sans répit les tristes cheminées
Fument, et que de suie une errante prison
Éteigne dans l'horreur de ses noires traînées
Le soleil se mourant jaunâtre à l'horizon!

—Le Ciel est mort. —Vers toi, j'accours! donne, ô matière,
L'oubli de l'Idéal cruel et du Péché
A ce martyr qui vient partager la litière
Où le bétail heureux des hommes est couché,

Will dip its tranquil horn in the water's glassy sheet
Not far from three long emerald eyelashes—reeds.

HUBERT CREEKMORE

THE AZURE

The everlasting Azure's tranquil irony
Depresses, like the flowers indolently fair,
The powerless poet who damns his superiority
Across a sterile wilderness of aching Despair.

In flight, with eyes shut fast, I feel it scrutinize
With all the vehemence of some destructive remorse,
My empty soul. Where can I flee? What haggard night
Fling over, tatters, fling on this distressing scorn?

Oh fogs, arise! Pour your monotonous ashes down
In long-drawn rags of dust across the skies unreeling
To darkly drench the livid swamp of autumn days,
And fabricate of them a great and silent ceiling!

And you, emerge from Lethean pools and gather in
While rising through them, freight of mud and pallid reeds,
Sweet Boredom, to block up with a never weary hand
The great blue holes the birds maliciously have made. . . .

Still more! Unceasing let the dismal chimney-flues
Exude their smoke, and let the soot's nomadic prison
Extinguish in the horror of its blackened queues
The sun now fading yellow away on the horizon!

—The Sky is dead. —To you I run, Oh matter! bestow
Forgetfulness of Sin and of the cruel Ideal
Upon this martyr who comes to share the stable straw
On which the happy human herd lies down to sleep.

Car j'y veux, puisque enfin ma cervelle, vidée
Comme le pot de fard gisant au pied du mur,
N'a plus l'art d'attifer la sanglotante idée,
Lugubrement bâiller vers un trépas obscur . . .

En vain! l'Azur triomphe, et je l'entends qui chante
Dans les cloches. Mon âme, il se fait voix pour plus
Nous faire peur avec sa victoire méchante,
Et du métal vivant sort en bleus angélus!

Il roule par la brume, ancien et traverse
Ta notive agonie ainsi qu'un glaive sûr;
Où fuir dans la révolte inutile et perverse?
Je suis hanté. L'Azur! l'Azur! l'Azur! l'Azur!

BRISE MARINE

La chair est triste, hélas! et j'ai lu tous les livres.
Fuir! là-bas fuir! Je sens que des oiseaux sont ivres
D'être parmi l'écume inconnue et les cieux!
Rien, ni les vieux jardins reflétés par les yeux
Ne retiendra ce cœur qui dans la mer se trempe
Ô nuits! ni la clarté déserte de ma lampe
Sur le vide papier que la blancheur défend
Et ni la jeune femme allaitant son enfant.
Je partirai! Steamer blançant ta mâture,
Lève l'ancre pour une exotique nature!

Un Ennui, désolé par les cruels espoirs,
Croit encore à l'adieu suprême des mouchoirs!
Et, peut-être, les mâts, invitant les orages
Sont-ils de ceux qu'un vent penche sur les naufrages
Perdus, sans mâts, sans mâts, ni fertiles îlots . . .
Mais, ô mon cœur, entends le chant des matelots!

For there I long, because at last my mind, drained
As is a rouge-pot lying on a closet shelf,
No longer has the art of decking tearful plaints,
To yawn lugubrious toward a humble death . . .

But vainly! The Azure triumphs and I hear it sing
In bells. Dear Soul, it turns into a voice the more
To fright us by its wicked victory, and springs
Blue Angelus, out of the living metal core.

It travels ancient through the fog, and penetrates
Like an unerring blade your native agony;
Where flee in my revolt so useless and depraved?
For I am haunted! The Sky! The Sky! The Sky! The Sky!

HUBERT CREEKMORE

SEA BREEZE

How sad the flesh! and there's no more to read.
Escape, far off! I feel that somewhere birds
Are drunk to be amid strange spray and skies!
Nothing, not those old gardens eyes reflect
Can now restrain this heart steeped in the sea
Oh nights! nor the lone brightness of my lamp
On the blank paper which its whiteness shields
Nor the young wife, her baby at her breast.
I shall depart! Steamer with swaying masts,
Raise anchor for exotic wilderness!

Tedium, desolated by cruel hope,
Has faith still in great fluttering farewells!
And, it may be, the masts, inviting storms
Are of the sort that wind inclines to wrecks
Lost, with no mast, no mast, or verdant isle . . .
But listen, oh my heart, the sailors sing!

PETER AND MARY ANN CAWS

SOUPIR

Mon âme vers ton front où rêve, ô calme sœur,
Un automne jonché de taches de rousseur,
Et vers le ciel errant de ton œil angélique
Monte, comme dans un jardin mélancolique,
Fidèle, un blanc jet d'eau soupire vers l'Azur!
—Vers l'Azur attendri d'Octobre pâle et pur
Qui mire aux grands bassins sa langueur infinie
Et laisse, sur l'eau morte où la fauve agonie
Des feuilles erre au vent et creuse un froid sillon,
Se traîner le soleil jaune d'un long rayon.

SIGH

Towards your brow where an autumn dreams
freckled with russet scatterings—
calm sister—and towards the sky,
wandering, of your angelic eye
my soul ascends: thus, white and true,
within some melancholy garden
a fountain sighs toward the Blue!
—Towards October's softened Blue
that pure and pale in the great pools
mirrors its endless lassitude
and, on dead water where the leaves
wind-strayed in tawny anguish cleave
cold furrows, lets the yellow sun
in one long lingering ray crawl on.

FREDERICK MORGAN

19

Autres poèmes

D'HÉRODIADE

NOURRICE

Tu vis ! ou vois-je ici l'ombre d'une princesse ?
A mes lèvres tes doigts et leurs bagues et cesse
De marcher dans un âge ignoré . . .

HÉRODIADE

                        Reculez.
Le blond torrent de mes cheveux immaculés
Quand il baigne mon corps solitaire le glace
D'horreur, et mes cheveux que la lumière enlace
Sont immortels. Ô femme, un baiser me tûrait
Si la beauté n'était la mort . . .
                      Par quel attrait
Menée et quel matin oublié des prophètes
Verse, sur les lointains mourants, ses tristes fêtes,
Le sais-je ? tu m'as vue, ô nourrice d'hiver,
Sous la lourde prison de pierres et de fer
Où de mes vieux lions traînent les siècles fauves
Entrer, et je marchais, fatale, les mains sauves,
Dans le parfum désert de ces anciens rois:
Mais encore as-tu vu quels furent mes effrois ?
Je m'arrête rêvant aux exils, et j'effeuille,
Comme près d'un bassin dont le jet d'eau m'accueille
Les pâles lys qui sont en moi, tandis qu'épris
De suivre du regard les languides débris
Descendre, à travers ma rêverie, en silence,
Les lions, de ma robe écartent l'indolence
Et regardent mes pieds qui calmeraient la mer.
Calme, toi, les frissons de ta sénile chair,

Other Poems

HERODIADE

NURSE

You're living! Or do I see the shadow of a princess?
Let me kiss your fingers and their rings, and may you
Walk no longer in an age ignored . . .

HERODIADE

                                   Draw back.
The blond torrent of my immaculate hair
Bathing my lonely body, freezes it
With horror, and my hair enlaced with light
Is deathless. Woman, a kiss might kill me,
Were not beauty death . . .
                             By what attraction
Drawn and what morning the prophets have forgotten
Inundates the dying distance with its sad festivals,
Do I ever know? You saw me, wintry nurse,
Deep in the heavy prison of stone and iron
Where tawny centuries hang from my old lions,
Descend, and I walked, doomed with hands unharmed,
Through the desert perfume of those former kings:
But did you see then what my terrors were?
I stop, dreaming of exile, and strip away the petals
As if near pools whose fountains welcome me,
From the pale lilies within me, while enraptured
To follow with their eyes the languid fragments
Falling, through my reverie, in the silence,
The lions disperse the indolence of my robes
And gaze upon my feet which would becalm the sea.
Restrain the shivering of your senile flesh,

Viens et ma chevelure imitant les manières
Trop farouches qui font votre peur des crinières,
Aide-moi, puisqu'ainsi tu n'oses plus me voir,
A me peigner nonchalamment dans un miroir.

NOURRICE

Sinon la myrrhe gaie en ses bouteilles closes,
De l'essence ravie aux vieillesses de roses,
Voulez-vous, mon enfant, essayer la vertu
Funèbre?

HÉRODIADE

Laisse là ces parfums! ne sais-tu
Que je les hais, nourrice, et veux-tu que je sente
Leur ivresse noyer ma tête languissante?
Je veux que mes cheveux qui ne sont pas des fleurs
A répandre l'oubli des humaines douleurs,
Mais de l'or, à jamais vierge des aromates,
Dans leurs éclairs cruels et dans leurs pâleurs mates
Observent la froideur stérile du métal,
Vous ayant reflétés, joyaux du mur natal,
Armes, vases depuis ma solitaire enfance.

NOURRICE

Pardon! l'âge effaçait, reine, votre défense
De mon esprit pâli comme un vieux livre ou noir . . .

HÉRODIADE

Assez! Tiens devant moi ce miroir.
                              Ô miroir!
Eau froide par l'ennui dans ton cadre gelée,
Que de fois et pendant des heures, désolée
Des songes et cherchant mes souvenirs qui sont

Come, and my hair resembling the too wild ways
Of the manes you are afraid of,
Help me, since you cannot bear the sight,
To comb it before the mirror, nonchalant.

NURSE

If not bright myrrh inside its bottles sealed,
Some essence ravished from the age of roses . . .
Will you, my child, not try its somber
Virtue?

HERODIADE

                    Leave those perfumes! Don't you know
That I abhor them, nurse, and would you have me feel
Their drunken raptures drown my languishing head?
I wish my hair, not being flowers
To exhale forgetfulness of human sorrows,
But rather gold, forever pure of aromatics,
In all its cruel flashes and dull pallors,
Conforming to that metal's barren cold,
Having reflected you, jewels of native walls,
Armor, vessels, since my childhood's solitude.

NURSE

Forgive me! Age, my queen, erased your interdiction
From my mind grown pale as an old book, or dark . . .

HERODIADE

Enough! Hold this mirror for me.
                    Oh mirror!
Cold water by weariness frozen in your frame,
How many times and hour by hour, distressed
By dreams and seeking my memories which are

Comme des feuilles sous ta glace au trou profond,
Je m'apparus en toi comme une ombre lointaine,
Mais, horreur! des soirs, dans ta sévère fontaine,
J'ai de mon rêve épars connu la nudité!

Nourrice, suis-je belle?

NOURRICE

                              Un astre, en vérité
Mais cette tresse tombe . . .

HÉRODIADE

                              Arrête dans ton crime
Qui refroidit mon sang vers sa source, et réprime
Ce geste, impiété fameuse : ah! conte-moi
Quel sûr démon te jette en le sinistre émoi,
Ce baiser, ces parfums offerts et, le dirai-je?
Ô mon cœur, cette main encore sacrilège,
Car tu voulais, je crois, me toucher, sont un jour
Qui ne finira pas sans malheur sur la tour . . .
Ô jour qu'Hérodiade avec effroi regarde!

NOURRICE

Temps bizarre, en effet, de quoi le ciel vous garde!
Vous errez, ombre seule et nouvelle fureur,
Et regardant en vous précoce avec terreur:
Mais toujours adorable autant qu'une immortelle
Ô mon enfant, et belle affreusement et telle
Que . . .

HÉRODIADE

Mais n'allais-tu pas me toucher?

Like leaves beneath the deep hollow of your ice,
I saw myself in you like a distant shadow,
But oh! Some evenings, dreadful in your harsh pool
I of my sparse dream perceived the nakedness!

Nurse, am I beautiful?

NURSE

Truly a star,
But this one tress is falling . . .

HERODIADE

Stop your crime
Which chills my blood to its well-springs, and check
That gesture, that supreme impiety: Tell me
What sure demon instills your sinister emotion?
That kiss, those offered perfumes and, dare I say it?
Oh heart, that still sacrilegious hand,
For you wanted, I think, to touch me, are a day
That will not end without disaster on the tower . . .
Oh day on which Herodiade's terror stares!

NURSE

Strange times, indeed, from which may heaven guard you!
You wander, solitary shade and unknown frenzy,
Still looking into yourself precocious with dread:
But ever to be adored as some immortal,
Oh my child, beautiful in horror and such
As . . .

HERODIADE

Yet were you not about to touch me?

... J'aimerais
Être à qui le destin réserve vos secrets.

HÉRODIADE

Oh! tais-toi!

NOURRICE

Viendra-t-il parfois?

HÉRODIADE

Étoiles pures,
N'entendez pas!

NOURRICE

Comment, sinon parmi d'obscures
Épouvantes, songer plus implacable encor
Et comme suppliant le dieu que le trésor
De votre grâce attend! et pour qui, dévorée
D'angoisses, gardez-vous la splendeur ignorée
Et le mystère vain de votre être?

HÉRODIADE

Pour moi.

NOURRICE

Triste fleur qui croît seule et n'a pas d'autre émoi
Que son ombre dans l'eau vue avec atonie.

NURSE

                     . . . . I would love
To serve the one for whom fate reserves your secrets.

HERODIADE

Be silent!

NURSE

        Will he come some day?

HERODIADE

                Pure stars,
Do not listen!

NURSE

        How, if not amid obscure
Affright, imagine more implacable still
And as a suitor the god for whom the treasure
Of your favor waits! and for whom, consumed
With anguish, do you keep the unknown splendor
And futile mystery of your being?

HERODIADE

           For myself.

NURSE

Sad flower that grows alone and feels no more
Than her own shade in water seen without response.

HÉRODIADE

Va, garde ta pitié comme ton ironie.

NOURRICE

Toutefois expliquez: oh! non, naïve enfant,
Décroîtra, quelque jour, ce dédain triomphant.

HÉRODIADE

Mais qui me toucherait, des lions respectée?
Du reste, je ne veux rien d'humain et, sculptée,
Si tu me vois les yeux perdus au paradis,
C'est quand je me souviens de ton lait bu jadis.

NOURRICE

Victime lamentable à son destin offerte!

HÉRODIADE

Oui, c'est pour moi, pour moi, que je fleuris, déserte!
Vous le savez, jardins d'améthyste, enfouis
Sans fin dans de savants abîmes éblouis,
Ors ignorés, gardant votre antique lumière
Sous le sombre sommeil d'une terre première,
Vous, pierres où mes yeux comme de purs bijoux
Empruntent leur clarté mélodieuse, et vous,
Métaux qui donnez à ma jeune chevelure
Une splendeur fatale et sa massive allure!
Quant à toi, femme née en des siècles malins
Pour la méchanceté des antres sibyllins
Qui parles d'un mortel! selon qui, des calices
De mes robes, arome aux farouches délices,
Sortirait le frisson blanc de ma nudité,
Prophétise que si le tiède azur d'été,

HERODIADE

Go on, keep for yourself your irony and your pity.

NURSE

Still, explain to me: no! naïve as you are,
Someday it will wither, triumphant scorn.

HERODIADE

But who would touch me, by the lions spared?
Besides, I want not human things, and if
You see me a statue, eyes lost in paradise,
It's when I recall your milk I drank so long ago.

NURSE

Pitiful victim offered to her destiny!

HERODIADE

Yes, it's for myself, myself, I flower, barren!
You know this, gardens of amethyst, buried
Endlessly in some knowing abysses dazzled,
Gold concealed, keeping your antique light
Beneath the somber sleep of a primeval soil,
You stones from which my eyes like purest jewels
Borrow their melodious brightness, and all
You metals which bestow on my youthful hair
A fatal splendor and its massive charm!
And you, woman born in evil times
To do the wickedness of sibylline caverns,
Who speaks of a mortal! who knew that, from the calyx
Of my robes, aroma of such fierce delights,
Would come from the white shiver of my nakedness,
Foretold how if the tepid azure of the summer,

Vers lui nativement la femme se dévoile,
Me voit dans ma pudeur grelottante d'étoile,
Je meurs!
                    J'aime l'horreur d'être vierge et je veux
Vivre parmi l'effroi que me font mes cheveux
Pour, le soir, retirée en ma couche, reptile
Inviolé sentir en la chair inutile
Le froid scintillement de ta pâle clarté
Toi qui te meurs, toi qui brûles de chasteté,
Nuit blanche de glaçons et de neige cruelle!
Et ta sœur solitaire, ô ma sœur éternelle,
Mon rêve montera vers toi: telle déjà,
Rare limpidité d'un cœur qui le songea,
Je me crois seule en ma monotone patrie
Et tout, autour de moi, vit dans l'idolâtrie
D'un miroir qui reflète en son calme dormant
Hérodiade au clair regard de diamant . . .
Ô charme dernier, oui! je le sens, je suis seule.

NOURRICE

Madame, allez-vous donc mourir!

HÉRODIADE

                              Non, pauvre aïeule,
Sois calme et, t'éloignant, pardonne à ce cœur dur,
Mais avant, si tu veux, clos les volets, l'azur
Séraphique sourit dans les vitres profondes,
Et je déteste, moi, le bel azur!
                                        Des ondes
Se bercent et, là-bas, sais-tu pas un pays
Où le sinistre ciel ait les regards haïs
De Vénus qui, le soir, brûle dans le feuillage;
J'y partirais.
                    Allume encore, enfantillage?
Dis-tu, ces flambeaux où la cire au feu léger

Before which woman by nature drops her veils,
Looks on my starry trembling modesty,
I die!
      I love the horror of being virgin and wish
To live amid the dread my hair makes me feel,
So that, at night, withdrawn into my bed, reptile
Inviolate I feel in my useless flesh
The cold scintillation of your pallid light
You who are dying, you who burn with chastity,
White night of icicles and cruel snow!
And your lonely sister, oh my eternal sister,
My dream will rise toward you: such already,
Rare clarity of a heart which dreamed it once,
I feel alone in my monotonous land
And all, about me, lives in the idolatry
Of a mirror reflecting in its sleeping calm
Herodiad whose bright gaze is a diamond . . .
Yes, last fascination! I feel it, I am alone.

NURSE

Madam, do you mean you are soon to die?

HERODIADE

                      No, poor ancient one,
Be calm, and, as you leave, forgive this hardened heart.
But first, please close the shutters, the blue sky
Smiles a seraph in the window's depths,
That blue detestable to me!
                  The waves
Lull, and yonder, do you know a land
Where the sinister sky has the hated look
Of Venus who burns in the evening foliage;
There would I go!
                And have them light, childish
Though it be, those torches where the wax in agile fire

Pleure parmi l'or vain quelque pleur étranger
Et . . .

NOURRICE

Maintenant?

HÉRODIADE

Adieu.
                                        Vous mentez, ô fleur nue
De mes lèvres!
                        J'attends une chose inconnue
Ou peut-être, ignorant le mystère et vos cris,
Jetez-vous les sanglots suprêmes et meurtris
D'une enfance sentant parmi les rêveries
Se séparer enfin ses froides pierreries.

L'APRÈS-MIDI D'UN FAUNE

Églogue

Le Faune

Ces nymphes, je les veux perpétuer.
                                        Si clair,
Leur incarnat léger, qu'il voltige dans l'air
Assoupi de sommeils touffus.

                        Aimai-je un rêve?
Mon doute, amas de nuit ancienne, s'achève
En maint rameau subtil, qui, demeuré les vrais
Bois mêmes, prouve, hélas! que bien seul je m'offrais

Weeps amid gold's vanity some strange tear
And then . . .

NURSE

What else?

HERODIADE

Goodbye.
                    You lie, oh naked flower
Of my lips.
            I await a thing unknown
Or perhaps, knowing not the mystery and your cries,
You utter the ultimate and wounded sobs
Of a childhood that feels among its reveries
Its frigid jewels draw apart at last.

HUBERT CREEKMORE

THE AFTERNOON OF A FAUN

Eclogue

The Faun

I would perpetuate these nymphs.
                    So clear,
The glow of them, so nimble in the air
Drowsiness encumbers—

                    Did I dream that love?
My doubt, the hoard of ancient night, divides
In subtle branches, which, the only woods
Remaining, prove, alas! that all alone

Pour triomphe la faute idéale de roses.
Réfléchissons . . .

       ou si les femmes dont tu gloses
Figurent un souhait de tes sens fabuleux!
Faune, l'illusion s'échappe des yeux bleus
Et froids, comme une source en pleurs, de la plus chaste
Mais, l'autre tout soupirs, dis-tu qu'elle contraste
Comme brise du jour chaude dans ta toison?
Que non! par l'immobile et lasse pâmoison
Suffoquant de chaleurs le matin frais s'il lutte,
Ne murmure point d'eau que ne verse ma flûte
Au bosquet arrosé d'accords; et le seul vent
Hors des deux tuyaux prompt à s'exhaler avant
Qu'il disperse le son dans une pluie aride,
C'est, à l'horizon pas remué d'une ride,
Le visible et serein souffle artificiel
De l'inspiration, qui regagne le ciel.

Ô bords siciliens d'un calme marécage
Qu'à l'envi de soleils ma vanité saccage,
Tacite sous les fleurs d'étincelles, CONTEZ
«*Que je coupais ici les creux roseaux domptés*
»*Par le talent; quand, sur l'or glauque de lointaines*
»*Verdures dédiant leur vigne à des fontaines,*
»*Ondoie une blancheur animale au repos:*
»*Et qu'au prélude lent où naissent les pipeaux*
»*Ce vol de cygnes, non! de naïades se sauve*
»*Ou plonge . . .*»

      Inerte, tout brûle dans l'heure fauve
Sans marquer par quel art ensemble détala
Trop d'hymen souhaité de qui cherche le *la:*
Alors m'éveillerai-je à la ferveur première,
Droit et seul, sous un flot antique de lumière,
Lys! et l'un de vous tous pour l'ingénuité.

I triumphed in the ideal fault of roses.
Reflect . . .

                    or if the women you malign
Configurate your fabled senses' wish!
That error flees before the chaste nymph's eyes,
As blue and cold, Faun, as a weeping stream.
But, for the other, would she not compare,
All sighs, to day's warm breezes in your fleece?
No! through this immobile lassitude
That stifles any protest from cool morning,
No water murmurs but the harmony
My flute pours on the grove; the only wind,
Quick to exhale from the two pipes, before
It dissipates the sound in arid rain,
Is, on the smooth horizon nothing moves,
The visible, serene, and artificial breath
Of inspiration, homing to the sky.

O you Sicilian shores of a calm marsh,
Which, rivaling suns, my vanity lays waste,
Silent beneath the flowers of light, RELATE
"I was cutting here the hollow reeds by talent
Mastered; against the distant glaucous gold
Of foliage offering its vines to streams,
Undulates animal whiteness in repose;
And, when the pipes are born in slow prelude,
A flight of swans, no! naiads hastens off
Or dives . . ."

                    Inert, all burns in the tawny hour
With no sign of the wiles by which escaped
That nuptial surfeit the musician sought.
Then to my native fervor I'll awake,
Upright, alone in ancient floods of light,
Lilies! and by my innocence your peer.

Autre que ce doux rien par leur lèvre ébruité,
Le baiser, qui tout bas des perfides assure,
Mon sein, vierge de preuve, atteste une morsure
Mystérieuse, due à quelque auguste dent;
Mais, bast! arcane tel élut pour confident
Le jonc vaste et jumeau dont sous l'azur on joue:
Qui, détournant à soi le trouble de la joue,
Rêve, dans un solo long, que nous amusions
La beauté d'alentour par des confusions
Fausses entre elle-même et notre chant crédule;
Et de faire aussi haut que l'amour se module
Évanouir du songe ordinaire de dos
Ou de flanc pur suivis avec mes regards clos,
Une sonore, vaine et monotone ligne.

Tâche donc, instrument des fuites, ô maligne
Syrinx, de refleurir aux lacs où tu m'attends!
Moi, de ma rumeur fier, je vais parler longtemps
Des déesses; et par d'idolâtres peintures,
A leur ombre enlever encore des ceintures:
Ainsi, quand des raisins j'ai sucé la clarté,
Pour bannir un regret par ma feinte écarté,
Rieur, j'élève au ciel d'été la grappe vide
Et, soufflant dans ses peaux lumineuses, avide
D'ivresse, jusqu'au soir je regarde au travers.

Ô nymphes, regonflons des SOUVENIRS divers.
«*Mon œil, trouant les joncs, dardait chaque encolure*
»*Immortelle, qui noie en l'onde sa brûlure*
»*Avec un cri de rage au ciel de la forêt;*
»*Et le splendide bain de cheveux disparaît*
»*Dans les clartés et les frissons, ô pierreries!*
»*J'accours; quand, à mes pieds, s'entrejoignent (meurtries*
»*De la langueur goûtée à ce mal d'être deux)*
»*Des dormeuses parmi leurs seuls bras hasardeux;*
»*Je les ravis, sans les désenlacer, et vole*

Save this sweet nothing rumored by their lips,
The kiss, mute witness to their perfidy,
Untouched by any proof, my chest reveals
Mysterious marks of sacramental teeth:
Enough! if such arcana deign to speak,
It is through vast twin reeds played under heaven,
Which, turning to themselves the cheek's emotion,
In an endless solo, dream that we amused
The beauty here around us, foolishly
Equating it with our own credulous song;
And of abstracting from the banal vision,
Contours of back or breast traced by closed eyes,
As high as love itself can modulate,
A sonorous, futile, uninflected line.

Try then, malicious Syrinx, instrument
Of flight, to flower anew beside our lakes!
As for me, proud of my voice, I'll speak at length
Of those divinities and by idolatrous
Depictions strip yet more veils from their shade.
Thus, when I've sucked the brightness out of grapes,
To chase regret deflected by my feint,
I lift the empty cluster to the sky,
Laughing, and, wild to be drunk, inflate
The shining skins and look through them till night.

O nymphs, let us inflate our MEMORIES.
"Piercing the reeds, my gaze stabs deathless
Throats, which drown their burning in the wave
With cries of outrage to the forest sky;
The splendid shower of tresses disappears
In a shimmering of precious gems! I lunge;
And there, entangled at my feet (cast down
By languor in the pain of being two)
Lie sleeping nymphs, at risk in their embrace;
I carry them off, still intertwined, and fly

»*A ce massif, haï par l'ombrage frivole,*
»*De roses tarissant tout parfum au soleil,*
»*Où notre ébat au jour consumé soit pareil.*»
Je t'adore, courroux des vierges, ô délice
Farouche du sacré fardeau nu qui se glisse
Pour fuir ma levre en feu buvant, comme un éclair
Tressaille! la frayeur secrète de la chair:
Des pieds de l'inhumaine au cœur de la timide
Que délaisse à la fois une innocence, humide
De larmes folles ou de moins tristes vapeurs.
«*Mon crime, c'est d'avoir, gai de vaincre ces peurs*
»*Traîtresses, divisé la touffe échevelée*
»*De baisers que les dieux gardaient si bien mêlée:*
»*Car, à peine j'allais cacher un rire ardent*
»*Sous les replis heureux d'une seule (gardant*
»*Par un doigt simple, afin que sa candeur de plume*
»*Se teignît à l'émoi de sa sœur qui s'allume,*
»*La petite, naïve et ne rougissant pas:)*
»*Que de mes bras, défaits par de vagues trépas,*
»*Cette proie, à jamais ingrate se délivre*
»*Sans pitié du sanglot dont j'étais encore ivre.*»

Tant pis! vers le bonheur d'autres m'entraîneront
Par leur tresse nouée aux cornes de mon front:
Tu sais, ma passion, que, pourpre et déjà mûre,
Chaque grenade éclate et d'abeilles murmure;
Et notre sang, épris de qui le va saisir,
Coule pour tout l'essaim éternel du désir.
A l'heure où ce bois d'or et de cendres se teinte
Une fête s'exalte en la feuillée éteinte:
Etna! c'est parmi toi visité de Vénus
Sur ta lave posant ses talons ingénus,
Quand tonne un somme triste ou s'épuise la flamme.
Je tiens la reine!

                    O sûr châtiment. . .
                                   Non, mais l'âme

To that high garden frivolous shadow scorns,
Where roses yield their fragrance to the sun
And, like the day, our sport may be consumed."
I love you, wrath of virgins, savage bliss—
The sacred naked burden as it writhes
To flee the fiery lightning of my lips,
While, from the cruel one's feet to the shy one's heart,
I drink the secret terror of the flesh;
And innocence, all moist with frenzied tears
Or with less woeful vapors, quits them both.
"Gay with the conquest of those treacherous fears,
I sinned when I divided that disheveled
Bouquet of kisses mingled by the gods;
For, as I moved to hide an ardent laugh
Deep amid joyous curves (and only held
By one sole finger, that her sister's kindling
Might lend its color to her downy whiteness,
The little one, unblushing and naive)
Then, from my arms, undone as if by death,
This prey, ungrateful to the end, breaks free,
Spurning the sob that kept me drunken still."

Who cares! their tresses knotted on my horns,
Others will draw me on toward happiness.
You know, my passion, that, crimson now and ripe,
Pomegranates burst in a hum of bees:
Our blood, enamored of its tyrant, flows
For the eternal swarming of desire.
When these woodlands take the hues of ash and gold,
Rejoicing quickens in the darkened leaves:
Etna! in your midst, where Venus comes,
Touching your lava with ingenuous feet,
When thunders sorry sleep or the flame burns dry.
I hold the queen!

                    Sure punishment . . .

                              No, the soul

·

De paroles vacante et ce corps alourdi
Tard succombent au fier silence de midi :
Sans plus il faut dormir en l'oubli du blasphème,
Sur le sable altéré gisant et comme j'aime
Ouvrir ma bouche à l'astre efficace des vins !

Couple, adieu ; je vais voir l'ombre que tu devins.

SAINTE

A la fenêtre recelant
Le santal vieux qui se dédore
De sa viole étincelant
Jadis avec flûte ou mandore,

Est la Sainte pâle étalant
Le livre vieux qui se déplie
Du Magnificat ruisselant
Jadis selon vêpre et complie :

A ce vitrage d'ostensoir
Que frôle une harpe par l'Ange
Formée avec son vol du soir
Pour la délicate phalange

Du doigt que, sans le vieux santal
Ni le vieux livre, elle balance
Sur le plumage instrumental,
Musicienne du silence.

Empty of words and this now torpid flesh
To noon's proud silence all too late succumb.
I must forget that blasphemy in sleep,
Laid out on thirsty sand, mouth open wide—
Oh, delight!—to wine's effectual star.

Couple, farewell; I'll see the shade that you became.

PATRICIA TERRY AND MAURICE Z. SHRODER

SAINT

At the window ledge concealing
The ancient sandalwood gold-flaking
Of her viol dimly twinkling
Long ago with flute or mandore,

Stands the pallid Saint displaying
The ancient missal page unfolding
At the Magnificat outpouring
Long ago for vesper and compline:

At that monstrance glazing lightly
Brushed now by a harp the Angel
Fashioned in his evening flight
Just for the delicate finger

Tip which, lacking the ancient missal
Or ancient sandalwood, she poises
On the instrumental plumage,
Musician of silence.

HUBERT CREEKMORE

AUTRE ÉVENTAIL

de Mademoiselle Mallarmé

Ô rêveuse, pour que je plonge
Au pur délice sans chemin,
Sache, par un subtil mensonge,
Garder mon aile dans ta main.

Une fraîcheur de crépuscule
Te vient à chaque battement
Dont le coup prisonnier recule
L'horizon délicatement.

Vertige! voici que frissonne
L'espace comme un grand baiser
Qui, fou de naître pour personne,
Ne peut jaillir ni s'apaiser.

Sens-tu le paradis farouche
Ainsi qu'un rire enseveli
Se couler du coin de ta bouche
Au fond de l'unanime pli!

Le sceptre des rivages roses
Stagnants sur les soirs d'or, ce l'est,
Ce blanc vol fermé que tu poses
Contre le feu d'un bracelet.

ANOTHER FAN

of Mademoiselle Mallarmé

Oh dreamer, that I may plunge
Pathless to pure delight,
Learn by a subtle lie
To keep my wing in your hand.

A twilight coolness comes
Upon you with each beat
Whose caged stroke lightly
Thrusts the horizon back.

Now feel space shivering
Dizzy, some great kiss
Which, wild to be born in vain,
Cannot break forth or rest.

Can you feel paradise
Shy as a buried laugh, slip
From the corner of your mouth
Down the concerted fold!

The scepter of pink shores
Stagnant on golden eves is
This white shut flight you pose
Against a bracelet's fire.

PETER AND MARY ANN CAWS

Plusieurs Sonnets

"QUAND L'OMBRE MENAÇA
DE LA FATALE LOI . . ."

Quand l'ombre menaça de la fatale loi
Tel vieux Rêve, désir et mal de mes vertèbres,
Affligé de périr sous les plafonds funèbres
Il a ployé son aile indubitable en moi.

Luxe, ô salle d'ébène où, pour séduire un roi
Se tordent dans leur mort des guirlandes célèbres,
Vous n'êtes qu'un orgueil menti par les ténèbres
Aux yeux du solitaire ébloui de sa foi.

Oui, je sais qu'au lointain de cette nuit, la Terre
Jette d'un grand éclat l'insolite mystère,
Sous les siècles hideux qui l'obscurcissent moins.

L'espace à soi pareil qu'il s'accroisse ou se nie
Roule dans cet ennui des feux vils pour témoins
Que s'est d'un astre en fête allumé le génie.

"LE VIERGE, LE VIVACE
ET LE BEL AUJOURD'HUI . . ."

Le vierge, le vivace et le bel aujourd'hui
Va-t-il nous déchirer avec un coup d'aile ivre
Ce lac dur oublié que hante sous le givre
Le transparent glacier des vols qui n'ont pas fui!

Un cygne d'autrefois se souvient que c'est lui
Magnifique mais qui sans espoir se délivre

Several Sonnets

"WHEN SHADOW THREATENED
WITH THE FATAL LAW . . ."

When shadow threatened with the fatal law
One old Dream, desire and pain of my spine,
Grieved at perishing beneath ceilings funereal,
It folded its indubitable wing within me.

Luxury, O ebony room where, to charm a king,
Celebrated garlands writhe in their death,
You are but a proud lie spoken by darkness
In the eyes of the lone man dazzled by his faith.

Yes, I know that, far in deep night, the Earth
Casts with great brilliance the strange mystery
Under the hideous centuries that darken it less.

Space ever alike if it grow or deny itself
Rolls in that boredom vile fires as witnesses
That genius has been lit with a festive star.

JAMES LAWLER

"WILL NEW AND ALIVE
THE BEAUTIFUL TODAY . . ."

Will new and alive the beautiful today
Shatter with a blow of drunken wing
This hard lake, forgotten, haunted under rime
By the transparent glacier, flights unflown!

A swan of long ago remembers now that he,
Magnificent but lost to hope, is doomed

Pour n'avoir pas chanté la région où vivre
Quand du stérile hiver a resplendi l'ennui.

Tout son col secouera cette blanche agonie
Par l'espace infligé à l'oiseau qui le nie,
Mais non l'horreur du sol où le plumage est pris.

Fantôme qu'à ce lieu son pur éclat assigne,
Il s'immobilise au songe froid de mépris
Que vêt parmi l'exil inutile le Cygne.

"VICTORIEUSEMENT FUI LE SUICIDE BEAU . . ."

Victorieusement fui le suicide beau
Tison de gloire, sang par écume, or, tempête !
Ô rire si là-bas une pourpre s'apprête
A ne tendre royal que mon absent tombeau.

Quoi ! de tout cet éclat pas même le lambeau
S'attarde, il est minuit, à l'ombre qui nous fête
Excepté qu'un trésor présomptueux de tête
Verse son caressé nonchaloir sans flambeau,

La tienne si toujours le délice ! la tienne
Oui seule qui du ciel évanoui retienne
Un peu de puéril triomphe en t'en coiffant

Avec clarté quand sur les coussins tu la poses
Comme un casque guerrier d'impératrice enfant
Dont pour te figurer il tomberait des roses.

For having failed to sing the realms of life
When the ennui of sterile winter gleamed.

His neck will shake off the white torment space
Inflicts upon the bird for his denial,
But not this horror, plumage trapped in ice.

Phantom by brilliance captive to this place,
Immobile, he assumes disdain's cold dream,
Which, in his useless exile, robes the Swan.

PATRICIA TERRY AND MAURICE Z. SHRODER

"VICTORIOUSLY FROM BEAUTIFUL SUICIDE HAVING FLED . . ."

Victoriously from beautiful suicide having fled
Ember of glory, blood through foam, gold, storm!
Oh laughing if out yonder a scarlet spreads
To drape regal only my absent tomb.

But look! of all that luster not even a shred
Lingers, midnight now, where the dark invites
Save that a presumptuous treasure of the head
Pours its caressed indolence without torch-light,

Yours always such a delight! And only yours
Oh yes that of a vanished heaven keeps
A trifling triumph by dressing those coiffures

With radiance when on the pillows you lie asleep
Like an infant queen in martial helmet tall
From which to image you roses should fall.

HUBERT CREEKMORE

"SES PURS ONGLES TRÈS HAUT DÉDIANT LEUR ONYX"

Ses purs ongles très haut dédiant leur onyx,
L'Angoisse, ce minuit, soutient, lampadophore,
Maint rêve vespéral brûlé par le Phénix
Que ne recueille pas de cinéraire amphore.

Sur les crédences, au salon vide: nul ptyx,
Aboli bibelot d'inanité sonore,
(Car le Maître est allé puiser des pleurs au Styx
Avec ce seul objet dont le Néant s'honore).

Mais proche la croisée au nord vacante, un or
Agonise selon peut-être le décor
Des licornes ruant du feu contre une nixe,

Elle, défunte nue en le miroir, encor
Que, dans l'oubli fermé par le cadre, se fixe
De scintillations sitôt le septuor.

"THE ONYX OF HER PURE NAILS OFFERED HIGH . . ."

The onyx of her pure nails offered high,
Lampadephore at midnight, Anguish bears
Many a twilight dream the Phoenix burned
To ashes gathered by no amphora.

On the credence, in the empty room: no ptyx,
Curio of vacuous sonority, extinct
(The Master's gone to dip tears from the Styx
With that unique delight of Nothingness).

But near the vacant northern window, gold
Expires, conformed perhaps to the motif
Of unicorn flames rearing at a nymph,

She, in the mirror, nude, defunct, although
Within the framed oblivion at once
Appears, all scintillation, the Septet.

PATRICIA TERRY AND MAURICE Z. SHRODER

Hommages et tombeaux

LE TOMBEAU D'EDGAR POE

Tel qu'en Lui-même enfin l'éternité le change,
Le Poëte suscite avec un glaive nu
Son siècle épouvanté de n'avoir pas connu
Que la mort triomphait dans cette voix étrange!

Eux, comme un vil sursaut d'hydre oyant jadis l'ange
Donner un sens plus pur aux mots de la tribu
Proclamèrent très haut le sortilège bu
Dans le flot sans honneur de quelque noir mélange.

Du sol et de la nue hostiles, ô grief!
Si notre idée avec ne sculpte un bas-relief
Dont la tombe de Poe éblouissante s'orne,

Calme bloc ici-bas chu d'un désastre obscur,
Que ce granit du moins montre à jamais sa borne
Aux noirs vols du Blasphème épars dans le futur.

LE TOMBEAU DE CHARLES BAUDELAIRE

Le temple enseveli divulgue par la bouche
Sépulcrale d'égout bavant boue et rubis
Abominablement quelque idole Anubis
Tout le museau flambé comme un aboi farouche

Ou que le gaz récent torde la mèche louche
Essuyeuse on le sait des opprobres subis

Homages and Tombs

THE TOMB OF EDGAR POE

As into Himself at last eternity changes him
The Poet wakens with a naked sword
His century dismayed not to have known
That death was triumphant in this strange voice!

Like a Hydra's vile spasm once hearing the angel
Give a purer sense to the words of the tribe
They proclaimed with loud cries the sortilege drunk
From the dishonored depths of some black brew.

From hostile soil and cloud, alas,
If our concept does not sculpt a bas-relief
To ornament the dazzling tomb of Poe,

Calm block here fallen from a dark disaster,
Let this granite at least mark bounds forever
To the dark flights of Blasphemy dispersed in the future.

MARY ANN CAWS

THE TOMB OF CHARLES BAUDELAIRE

The buried temple through the sewer's dark
Sepulchral mouth that drools out mud and rubies
Reveals abominably some god Anubis
His whole snout blazing with a savage bark

Or should the new gas twist the filthy wick
Assuager so well known of shame long brooded

Il allume hagard un immortel pubis
Dont le vol selon le réverbère découche

Quel feuillage séché dans les cités sans soir
Votif pourra bénir comme elle se rasseoir
Contre le marbre vainement de Baudelaire

Au voile qui la ceint absente avec frissons
Celle son Ombre même un poison tutélaire
Toujours à respirer si nous en périssons.

TOMBEAU DE PAUL VERLAINE

Anniversaire—Janvier 1897

Le noir roc courroucé que la bise le roule
Ne s'arrêtera ni sous de pieuses mains
Tâtant sa ressemblance avec les maux humains
Comme pour en bénir quelque funeste moule.

Ici presque toujours si le ramier roucoule
Cet immatériel deuil opprime de maints
Nubiles plis l'astre mûri des lendemains
Dont un scintillement argentera la foule.

Qui cherche, parcourant le solitaire bond
Tantôt extérieur de notre vagabond—
Verlaine? Il est caché parmi l'herbe, Verlaine

A ne surprendre que naïvement d'accord
La lèvre sans y boire ou tarir son haleine
Un peu profond ruisseau calomnié la mort.

It kindles haggard an immortal pubis
Whose flight along the street lamps loiters awake

What dried leaves in the towns without the prayer
Of night can bless as it again must cling
In vain against the marble of Baudelaire

In veils that wreathe its absence with shimmering
His own Shade this a guardian poison still
To breathe in always even though it kill.

HUBERT CREEKMORE

TOMB OF PAUL VERLAINE

Anniversary—January 1897

The dark rock angry that the high wind rolls
It will not linger even for pious hands
Feeling its likeness with the woes of man
As if to bless in it some fatal mould.

Here often if the ring-dove coos its song
This insubstantial grief burdens with scores
Of nubile folds the future's ripened star
Whose scintillation will silvercoat the throng.

Who seeks, pursuing the solitary leap
Till now external of our vagabond—
Verlaine? He's hidden in the grass, Verlaine

Amazing only as naively agreed
His lips not drinking there or ceasing breath
A stream not very deep and slandered death.

HUBERT CREEKMORE

53

HOMMAGE À RICHARD WAGNER

Le silence déjà funèbre d'une moire
Dispose plus qu'un pli seul sur le mobilier
Que doit un tassement du principal pilier
Précipiter avec le manque de mémoire.

Notre si vieil ébat triomphal du grimoire,
Hiéroglyphes dont s'exalte le millier
A propager de l'aile un frisson familier!
Enfouissez-le-moi plutôt dans une armoire.

Du souriant fracas originel haï
Entre elles de clartés maîtresses a jailli
Jusque vers un parvis né pour leur simulacre,

Trompettes tout haut d'or pâmé sur les vélins,
Le dieu Richard Wagner irradiant un sacre
Mal tu par l'encre même en sanglots sibyllins.

UN TOMBEAU POUR ANATOLE (*extraits*)

17.

père et mère se
  promettant de
  n'avoir pas d'autre
  enfant
    —fosse creusée par lui
    vie cesse là

HOMAGE TO RICHARD WAGNER

The silence now funereal of a pall
Spreads more than one fold on this furniture
Which must with lack of memory bestir
A collapsing of the central pedestal.

Our old triumphal sport of the magic book,
Hieroglyphs exciting many still
To spread with wings a too familiar thrill!—
Bury it rather in a cupboard-nook.

From smiling loathed original uproar
To those of mighty splendors has sprung forth
In temple courtyard for their image fashioned,

Loud golden horns aswoon on vellum, the god
Richard Wagner glittering consecration
Ill silenced even by ink in sibylline sobs.

HUBERT CREEKMORE

A TOMB FOR ANATOLE (*excerpts*)

17.

father and mother
 vowing
 to have no other
child
   —grave dug by him
   life ends here

37.

temps de la
    chambre vide
—

    jusqu'à ce qu'on
      l'ouvre
peut-être tout
    suivre ainsi
     (moralement)

87.

ô terre—tu n'as
   pas une plante
—à quoi bon —
--moi qui
   t'honore—

bouquets
    vaine beauté

190.

non — je ne
laisserai pas
   le néant
    père — — — je
sens le néant
   m'envahir

37.

time of the
 empty room
—

 until we
  open it
perhaps all
 follows from this
  (morally)

87.

o earth—you do not
 grow anything
—pointless—
—I who
 honor you—

bouquets
 vain beauty

190.

 no—I will not
give up
 nothingness
  ———

 father — — — I
feel nothingness
 invade me

PAUL AUSTER

Autres poèmes et sonnets

"UNE DENTELLE S'ABOLIT . . ."

Une dentelle s'abolit
Dans le doute du Jeu suprême
A n'entr'ouvrir comme un blasphème
Qu'absence éternelle de lit.

Cet unanime blanc conflit
D'une guirlande avec la même,
Enfui contre la vitre blême
Flotte plus qu'il n'ensevelit.

Mais, chez qui du rêve se dore
Tristement dort une mandore
Au creux néant musicien

Telle que vers quelque fenêtre
Selon nul ventre que le sien,
Filial on aurait pu naître.

"MES BOUQUINS REFERMÉS
SUR LE NOM DE PAPHOS . . ."

Mes bouquins refermés sur le nom de Paphos,
Il m'amuse d'élire avec le seul génie
Une ruine, par mille écumes bénie
Sous l'hyacinthe, au loin, de ses jours triomphaux.

Coure le froid avec ses silences de faux,

Other Poems and Sonnets

"LACE PASSES INTO NOTHINGNESS . . ."

Lace passes into nothingness,
With the ultimate Gamble in doubt,
In blasphemy revealing just
Eternal absence of any bed.

This concordant enmity
Of a white garland and the same,
In flight against the pallid glass,
Hovers and does not enshroud.

But where, limned gold, the dreamer dwells,
There sleeps a mournful mandola,
Its deep lacuna source of song,

Of a kind that toward some window,
Formed by that belly or none at all,
Filial, one might have been born.

PATRICIA TERRY AND MAURICE Z. SHRODER

"WHEN MY OLD BOOKS ARE CLOSED ON PAPHOS' NAME . . ."

When my old books are closed on Paphos' name
I delight in choosing only in my mind,
A ruin, blessed by many a foam, beneath
The hyacinth, far off, of its triumphant time.

Let the cold run, silent as a scythe,

Je n'y hululerai pas de vide nénie
Si ce très blanc ébat au ras du sol dénie
A tout site l'honneur du paysage faux.

Ma faim qui d'aucuns fruits ici ne se régale
Trouve en leur docte manque une saveur égale:
Qu'un éclate de chair humain et parfumant!

Le pied sur quelque guivre où notre amour tisonne,
Je pense plus longtemps peut-être éperdument
A l'autre, au sein brûlé d'une antique amazone.

I shall not cry a bare complaint
Should this white sport on the ground deny
To any site the honor of the false scene.

My hunger feasting on no fruits here
Finds in their learned lack an equal taste:
Let one appear in human flesh and scent!

My foot on some serpent where our love fires the coals,
I think still longer, with passion perhaps,
Of that other, the seared breast of an ancient Amazon.

MARY ANN CAWS

Prose Poems

THE SHUDDER OF WINTER

The old Saxony clock, which is slow, and which strikes thirteen amid its flowers and gods, to whom did it belong? Thinkest that it came from Saxony by the mail coaches of old time?

(Singular shadows hang about the worn-out panes.)

And thy Venetian mirror, deep as a cold fountain in its banks of tarnished gilt work; what is reflected there? Ah! I am sure that more than one woman bathed there in her beauty's sin: and, perhaps, if I looked long enough, I should see a naked phantom.

Wicked one, thou often sayest wicked things.

(I see the spiders' webs above the lofty windows.)

Our wardrobe is very old; see how the fire reddens its sad panels! the weary curtains are as old, and the tapestry on the armchairs stripped of paint, and the old engravings and all these old things. Does it not seem to thee that even these blue birds are discoloured by time?

(Dream not of the spiders' webs that tremble above the lofty windows.)

Thou lovest all that, and that is why I live by thee. When one of my poems appeared, didst thou not desire, my sister, whose looks are full of yesterdays, the words, "the grace of faded things"? New objects displease thee; thee also do they frighten with their loud boldness, and thou feelest as if thou shouldest use them—a difficult thing indeed to do, for thou hast no taste for action.

Come, close thy old German almanack that thou readest with attention, though it appeared more than a hundred years ago, and the Kings it announces are all dead, and, lying on this antique carpet, my head leaned upon thy charitable knees, on the pale robe, oh! calm child. I will speak with thee for hours; there are no fields, and the streets are empty. I will speak to thee of our furniture. . . . Thou art abstracted?

(The spiders' webs are shivering above the lofty windows.)

GEORGE MOORE

THE WHITE WATER-LILY

I had been rowing for a long time with a sweeping, rhythmical, drowsy stroke, my eyes within me fastened upon my utter forgetfulness of motion, while the laughter of the hour flowed round about. Immobility dozed everywhere so quietly that, when I was suddenly brushed by a dull sound which my boat half ran into, I could tell that I had stopped only by the quiet glittering of initials on the lifted oars. Then I was recalled to my place in the world of reality.

What was happening? Where was I?

To see to the bottom of my adventure I had to go back in memory to my early departure, in that flaming July, through the rapid opening and sleeping vegetation of an ever narrow and absentminded stream, my search for water flowers, and my intention of reconnoitring an estate belonging to the friend of a friend of mine, to whom I would pay my respects as best I could. No ribbon of grass had held me near any special landscape; all were left behind, along with their reflections in the water, by the same impartial stroke of my oars; and I had just now run aground on a tuft of reeds, the mysterious end of my travels, in the middle of the river. There, the river broadens out into a watery thicket and quietly displays the elegance of a pool, rippling like the hesitation of a spring before it gushes forth.

Upon closer examination, I discovered that this tuft of green tapering off above the stream concealed the single arch of a bridge which was extended on land by a hedge on either side surrounding a series of lawns. Then it dawned on me: this was simply the estate belonging to the unknown lady to whom I had come to pay my respects.

It was an attractive place for this time of year, I thought, and I could only sympathize with anyone who had chosen a retreat so watery and impenetrable. Doubtless she had made of this crystal surface an inner mirror to protect herself from the brilliant indiscretion of the afternoons. Now, I imagined, she must be approaching it; the silvery mist chilling the willow trees has just become her limpid glance, which is familiar with every leaf.

I conjured her up in her perfection and her purity.

Bending forward with an alertness prompted by my curiosity, and immersed in the spacious silence of the worlds still uncreated by my unknown lady, I smiled at the thought of the bondage she might lead me into. This was well symbolized by the strap which fastens the rower's shoe to the bottom of the boat; for we are always at one with the instrument of our magic spells.

"Probably just somebody . . ." I was about to say.

Then, suddenly, the tiniest sound made me wonder whether the dweller on this bank was hovering about me—perhaps by the river!—while I lingered there.

The walking stopped. Why?

Oh, subtle secret of feet as they come and go and lead my imagination on, and bend it to the desire of that dear shadow! She is hidden in cambric and in the lace of a skirt flowing on the ground, floating about heel and toe as if to surround her step before she takes it, as (with folds thrown back in a train) she walks forth with her cunning twin arrows.

Has she—herself the walker—a reason for standing there? And yet have I the right, on my side, to penetrate this mystery further by lifting my head above these reeds and waking from that deep imaginative drowse in which my clear vision has been veiled?

"Whatever your features may be, Madame (I whisper to myself), I sense that the instinctive, subtle charm created here by the sound of my arrival would be broken if I saw them—a charm not to be denied the explorer by the most exquisitely knotted of sashes, with its diamond buckle. An image as vague as this is self-sufficient; and it will not destroy the delight which has the stamp of generality, which permits and commands me to forget all real faces; for if I saw one (oh, don't bend yours here, don't let me see it on this ephemeral threshold where I reign supreme!), it would break the spell which is of another world."

I can introduce myself in my pirate dress and say that I happened here by chance.

Separate as we are, we are together. Now I plunge within this mingled intimacy, in this moment of waiting on the water; my reverie keeps her here in hesitation, better than visit upon visit could do. How many fruitless talks there would have to be—when I compare them to the one I have had, unheard—before we could find so intimate an understanding as we do now, while I listen along the level of the boat and the expanse of sand now silent!

The waiting moment lasts while I decide.

Oh, my dream, give counsel! What shall I do?

With a glance I shall gather up the virginal absence scattered through this solitude and steal away with it; just as, in memory of a special site, we pick one of those magical, still unopened waterlilies which suddenly spring up there and enclose, in their deep white, a nameless nothingness made of unbroken reveries, of happiness never to be—made of my breathing, now, as it stops for fear that she may show herself. Steal silently away, rowing bit by bit, so that the illusion may not be shattered by the stroke of oars, nor the plashing of the visible foam, unwinding behind me as I flee, reach the feet of any chance walker on the bank, nor bring with it the transparent resemblance of the theft I made of the flower of my mind.

But if, sensing something unusual, she was induced to appear (my Meditative lady, my Haughty, my Cruel, my Gay unknown), so much the worse for that ineffable face which I shall never know! For I executed my plan according to my rules: I pushed off, turned, and then skirted a river wave; and so, like a noble swan's egg fated never to burst forth in flight, I carried off my imaginary trophy, which bursts only with that exquisite absence of self which many a lady loves to pursue in summer along the paths of her park, as she stops sometimes and lingers by a spring which must be crossed or by a lake.

BRADFORD COOK

Sketched in the Theatre

THE MIME

Silence, sole luxury after rhymes, an orchestra only marking with its gold, its brushes with thought and dusk, the detail of its signification on a par with a stilled ode and which it is up to the poet, roused by a dare, to translate! the silence of an afternoon of music; I find it, with contentment, also, before the ever original reappearance of Pierrot or of the poignant and elegant mime Paul Margueritte.

Such is this *Pierrot Murderer of His Wife* composed and set down by himself, a mute soliloquy that the phantom, white as a yet unwritten page, holds in both face and gesture at full length to his soul. A whirlwind of naive or new reasons emanates, which it would be pleasing to seize upon with security: the esthetics of the genre situated closer to principles than any! nothing in this region of caprice foiling the direct simplifying instinct . . . This—"The scene illustrates but the idea, not any actual action, in a hymen (out of which flows Dream), tainted with vice yet sacred, between desire and fulfillment, perpetration and remembrance: here anticipating, there recalling, in the future, in the past, *under the false appearance of a present.* That is how the Mime operates, whose act is confined to a perpetual allusion without breaking the ice or the mirror: he thus sets up a medium, a pure medium, of fiction." Less than a thousand lines, the role, the one that reads, will instantly comprehend the rules as if placed before the stageboards, their humble depository. Surprise, accompanying the artifice of a notation of sentiments by unproffered sentences—that, in the sole case, perhaps, with authenticity, between the sheets and the eye there reigns a silence still, the condition and delight of reading.

BARBARA JOHNSON

HAMLET

Far removed from everything, autumnal Nature prepares Her Theater sublime and pure. She will not, in Her solitude, shed light upon essential miracles until the Poet, whose lucid eye alone can penetrate their meaning (and that meaning is the destiny of man), has been called back to ordinary cares and pleasures.

I am back again now, forgetting dead-leaf bitterness; and I should like to note down the impressions that a few of my friends and myself have had of rather banal Evenings which even the loneliest among us cannot fail to consider as he dresses for the theater. He does so in order to protract his feeling of uneasiness, well aware (because certain laws are still unfulfilled) that the extraordinary moment is no longer, or not yet, at hand.

.   .   .   .

> And now, oh child cut off from glory,
> You feel the wind in the absurd night,
> Upon your pale forehead as white as milk,
> Blowing your black feather
> And caressing you, Hamlet! oh young Hamlet!
> (Théodore de Banville)

That adolescent who vanished from us at the beginning of his life and who will always haunt lofty, pensive minds with his mourning is very present to me now as I see him struggling against the curse of having to appear. For that is precisely, uniquely the kind of character that Hamlet externalizes on the stage, in an intimate and occult tragedy; his name, even when posted, has a fascination for me, and for you who read it, which approaches anguish. I am thankful that chance has drawn me away from my imaginative and absent-minded vision of the theater of clouds and truth, brought me down to a human stage, and given me, as my first topic of discussion, what I consider to be *the* play. For had it become too quickly disaccustomed to the purple, violet, pink, and eternally gold horizon, my vision might easily have been offended. My relationship with the skies, which were my home, now ends; and my place in front of that screen of glory is not taken by any of my indelicately palpable contemporaries. (Farewell to the brilliance of that yearly holocaust which has flamed out to the proportions of all time, so that there may be no witness to its empty rite.) And now here comes *the prince of promise unfulfillable,* young shade of all of us; and therefore there is myth in him. The lonely drama that he plays! This walker in a labyrinth of agitation and grievance so prolongs its windings with his unfinishing of an unfinished act, that he sometimes seems to be the only reason for the existence of the stage and of the golden, almost moral, space which the stage protects. For remember! Here is the only plot in drama: the struggle, in man, between his dream and the fates allotted to his life by evil fortune.

It is true that the chief interest today lies in the interpretation; but of this it was impossible to speak without having first compared it to the concept of the play.

What I shall say now has been inspired by the leading actor.

Single-handedly, through divination, through an incomparable technical mastery, and also by virtue of his literary faith in the always unfailing and mysterious beauty of the role, he was able to weave some nameless evil spell which stole into the air of this imposing performance. I have no objection to the location of the magnificent site or to the sumptuous costumes which were worn, even though, according to the latest erudite craze, they are dated (but are they really?); and even though the choice of the Renaissance period (cleverly and mistily covered up by a touch of Northern fur) is detrimental to the original perspective of the legend. One result is that the characters are made to look like contemporaries of the dramatist. Hamlet himself avoids this mistake with the traditional scantiness of his dark dress, looking a little like a Goya. This work of Shakespeare is so well patterned on the theater of the mind alone—this being the prototype of all others—that it makes no difference whether or not it is adapted for modern production. What bothers me is something other than tiny details which are infinitely difficult to regulate, in any case, and debatable at best: that is, a quality of intelligence belonging exclusively to the Parisian location of Elsinore, or—to borrow the philosophers' language—the "error of the *Théâtre-Français*." But it is the error of no one person; and in this performance the élite company was duly acclaimed for its energetic attention to detail.

They certainly want to do Shakespeare, and they want to do him well. Talent, however, is not sufficient; there must be certain ingrained habits of understanding and interpretation. Here was Horatio, for example (although I am not particularly concerned with him), with something classical and Molièresque about him. Then Laertes (here I *am* concerned) played downstage and for his own sake, as if his travels and paltry twin griefs were of special interest. Even the finest of qualities must remain relatively unimportant in a story which dwells solely on an imaginary and somewhat abstract hero. Otherwise the reality of the atmosphere created by the symbolic Hamlet will be disintegrated like a curtain of mist. Actors, it must be so! For in the ideal stage performance, everything must be carried out in *obedience to a symbolic relationship of characters, either to themselves or to a single figure.* For example, an actor shows intensity and unstinting zest in a masterful rendition of Polonius, and turns him into the foolish, eager, senile steward of a merry tale. I do not entirely object to this. But in so doing he is forgetting an entirely different official whom I used to enjoy in retrospect: a figure I like to imagine as being cut out of a threadbare arras, like the one he must hide behind to die; a colorless, unsubstantial, aged clown whose almost weightless corpse, abandoned halfway through the play, has no importance save in the brusque and wild-eyed exclamation: "A rat!" Whoever hovers around an exceptional character such as Hamlet, is merely Hamlet himself. And, with his useless sword-point, the prophetic prince, destined to perish on the threshold of manhood, melancholically pushes that heap of garrulous nothingness off the path which he himself cannot follow—heap which he in turn might be, if he grew old. Ophelia, virgin child in the mind of the pitiful royal heir, was played in the modern conservatory style: she was natural, as the ingenues would have her; and rather than succumb to her songs, she preferred to use all the everyday knowledge of an experienced actress. She has a certain perfection in her tone, not without a grace of its own, which is evident in her performances and in her personality. And now, in my memory, beside the letters which spell out the name of Shakespeare, I find certain names flitting about which it would be sacrilegious even to shroud in silence, because we can divine them.

How great the power of Dreams is!

What exactly is that nameless, subtle, faded self-effacement (like the coloring of old fairy-tales) which is missing from the work of certain masters who like to make things plain, clear, and brand-new? Hamlet (a stranger everywhere) brings that quality to bear upon the hard and overly obtrusive, through the disquieting and funereal invasion of his presence. Whenever the French version of the play becomes a little too exclusively patterned, the actor restores things to their proper places; with a gesture, he exorcizes and neutralizes the pernicious influence of the *Théâtre-Français;* and, at the same time, breathes out the atmosphere of genius; all this he does with a masterful touch, because he has looked into this time-honored text with simplicity, as in a mirror. His charm lies entirely in a sort of disconsolate elegance, and lends a kind of cadence to his every start. Then there is the longing for his early and still unforgotten wisdom, despite the aberrations caused by the storm as it assails the delightful feather in his cap. Such, it would seem, is the distinctive characteristic and inventiveness in the acting of this man who, from an instinct which is sometimes obscure even to himself, draws forth the intuitions of the learned. In this way, it seems to me, he renders the morbid duality so typical of Hamlet: mad, yes, in outward appearance, whipped as he is in both directions by his duty; but oh! nonetheless, his eyes are still upon an image of himself within, and this he keeps intact—like an Ophelia still undrowned!—always prepared to get his balance back again. Jewel intact in the midst of chaos.

From the plastic and mental points of view, the tragedian, mime, and thinker is a prince of the dramatic art in his interpretation of Hamlet; and, above all, he gives us the Hamlet who has been bequeathed to contemporary minds. It was fitting, after the painful vigil of the Romantic period, that we should have at least one chance to see the essence of that magnificent daemon reach us; his bearing will not, perhaps, be understood in days to come, but the accomplishment remains. Solemnly, this actor has drawn a portrait which is immortal, lucid, somewhat composite and yet quite unified, and somehow authenticated by the seal of a supreme and timeless age; and he has given it to a future which will probably care nothing for it, but which, in any case, will be unable to alter it.

BRADFORD COOK

Variations on a Subject

CRISIS IN POETRY (*excerpts*)

. . . Each soul is a melody which must be picked up again, and the flute or the viola of everyone exists for that.

Late in coming, it seems to me, is the true condition or the possibility not just of expressing onself but of modulating oneself as one chooses.

Languages are imperfect in that although there are many, the supreme one is lacking: thinking is to write without accessories, or whispering, but since the immortal word is still tacit, the diversity of tongues on the earth keeps everyone from uttering the word which would be otherwise in one unique rendering, truth itself in its substance . . . *Only,* we must realize, *poetry would not exist;* philosophically, verse makes up for what languages lack, completely superior as it is.

. . .

The pure work implies the disappearance of the poet as speaker, yielding his initiative to words, which are mobilized by the shock of their difference; they light up with reciprocal reflections like a virtual stream of fireworks over jewels, restoring perceptible breath to the former lyric impulse, or the enthusiastic personal directing of the sentence.

. . .

One desire of my epoch which cannot be dismissed is to separate so as to attribute them differently the double state of the immediate or unrefined word on one hand, the essential one on the other.

. . .

What good is the marvel of transposing a fact of nature into its almost complete and vibratory disappearance with the play of the word, however, unless there comes forth from it, without the bother of a nearby or concrete reminder, the pure notion.

I say: a flower! and outside the oblivion to which my voice relegates any shape, insofar as it is something other than the calyx, there arises musically, as the very idea and delicate, the one absent from every bouquet.

MARY ANN CAWS

As for the Book

ACTION RESTRICTED

Several times a Colleague came to me, the same one, this other, to confide in me his need to act: what was he aiming at—since his approaching me announced on his part also, young as he was, the concern with creation, seemingly supreme, and success with words; I repeat, what did he mean exactly?

Unclenching your fists, breaking off with some sedentary dream, for a violent tête-à-tête with the idea, as when a fancy strikes one, or moving: but this generation seems not very concerned—even beyond its lack of interest in politics—with the desire for physical exertion. Except of course, with the monotony of winding along the pavement between one's shin bones, according to the machine at present in favor, the fiction of continuous dazzling speedway.

Acting, leaving this aside, and for the one who only smokes as a beginning, meant, oh visitor I understand you, philosophically to effect motion on many, which yields in return the happy thought that you, being the cause of it, therefore exist: no one is sure of that in advance. This can be accomplished in two ways: either in a lifetime of willing and ignoring it, until the explosion—that is thinking, or in the outpourings now in reach of the prudent grasp, the daily newspapers and their whirlwind, determining in them, in one sense, some strength—which several will dispute, whatever it is—with the immunity of no result.

As you like, according to disposition, plenitude, haste.

Your act is always applied to paper; for meditating without leaving any traces becomes evanescent, nor should instinct be exalted in some vehement and lost gesture that you sought.

To write—

The inkstand, crystal as a conscience, within its depths its drop of shadow relative to having something be: then take away the lamp.

You noticed, one does not write luminously on a dark field; the alphabet of stars alone, is thus indicated, sketched out or interrupted; man pursues black on white.

This pleat of somber lace which retains the infinite woven by a thousand, each according to the thread or the prolongation, its secret unknown, assembles distant interlacings where there sleeps some luxury to take account of—a ghoul, a knot, some foliage—and to present.

With the indispensable nothing of mystery, which remains, expressed little.

I do not know if the Host circumscribes perspicaciously his domain: it will please me to mark it out, and also certain conditions. The right to accomplish nothing exceptional, or lacking in vulgar bustle: anyone must pay for it by being omitted and, you might say, by death as a person. His exploits are committed while dreaming, so as to bother no one; but still their program is displayed for those who care nothing about it.

The writer must make himself, in the text, the spiritual actor either of his sufferings, those dragons he has nurtured, or of some happiness.

Floor, lamp, clouding of cloths and melting of mirrors, real even down to the exaggerated jerking of our gauzy form around the virile stature stopped upon one foot; a Place comes forth, a stage, the public enhancement of the spectacle of Self; there, through the mediation of light, flesh, and laughter, the sacrifice of personality made by the inspirer is complete; or else in some foreign resurrection, he is finished: his word from then on, reverberating and useless, is exhaled by the orchestral chimera.

A theater hall: he celebrates himself, anonymous, in the hero.

Everything as the playing out of festivals: a people bears witness to its transfiguration into truth.

Honor.

Be on the lookout for something similar—

Will it be recognized in these suspicious buildings detached by some banal excess from the common alignment, claiming to synthesize the miscellaneous bits of the neighborhood? If some facade in the forward-looking French taste makes an isolated apparition on some square, I salute it. Indifferent to what is uttered, in this place and that, as the flame with lowered tongues runs along the pipes.

Thus Action of the kind agreed upon, literary, does not transgress the Theater, limiting itself to representation—the immediate disappearance of the written. Let it end; in the street, somewhere else, the mask falls; I have nothing to do with the poet: perjure your verse, it is

gifted with only a feeble outer power. You preferred to feed the re-
mainder of intrigues entrusted to the individual. Why should I make it
clear for you, child, you know it just as I do, retaining no notion of it
except by some quality or lack which is childhood's alone; this point,
that everything, whether vehicle or investment, now offered to the ideal,
is contrary to it—almost a speculation on your modesty, for your silence—
or it is defective, not direct and legitimate in the sense that impulse
required just now, and it is tainted. Since uneasiness was never enough,
I shall certainly clarify, however many future digressions it may take,
this reciprocal contamination of work and means: but first was it not
good to express myself spaciously, as with a cigar in convolutions whose
vagueness, at the very least, traced its outline on the raw electric day-
light?

A delicate being has, or so I hope, suffered—

Outside, like the cry of space, the traveler perceives the whistle's
distress. "Probably," he persuades himself, "we are going through a
tunnel—*the epoch*—the last long one, snaking under the city to the all-
powerful train station of the virginal central palace, like a crown." The
underground passage will last (how impatient you are), as long as
your thoughtful preparation of the tall glass edifice wiped clean by
Justice in flight.

Suicide or abstention, doing nothing, why?—Time unique in the
world, since because of an event I have still to explain, there is no
Present, no—a present does not exist . . . Lack the Crowd declares in
itself, lack—of everything. Ill-informed anyone who would announce
himself his own contemporary, deserting, usurping with equal impu-
dence, when the past ceased and when a future is slow to come, or when
both are mingled perplexedly to cover up the gap. Except for the first
Paris editions supposed to divulge some faith in daily nothingness, inept
if the malady measures its duration by a fragment, important or not, of
a century.

So watch out and be there.

Poetry, consecration; trying out, lonely in its chaste crises, during the
other gestation as it continues.

Publish.

The Book, where the satisfied spirit dwells, in case of misunder-
standing, is obligated, by some struggle, to shake off the bulk of the

moment. Not personalized, the volume, from which one is separated as the author, does not demand that any reader approach it. You should know that as such, without any human accessories, it happens all alone; made, being. The hidden meaning stirs, and lays out a choir of pages.

No more arrogant denial of the moment, even in the celebrations: it is to be noticed that some chance forbids to dreams the materials to fight with, or favors a certain attitude.

You, Friend, must not be deprived of years because you parallel the deaf drudgery of the many, the case is strange: I ask you, without judging, for lack of sudden preambles, to treat my information as a madness, I admit it, rare. However, it is already modified by this wisdom, or this understanding, if that's all it is—risking on some surrounding condition, incomplete at the very least, certain extreme conclusions about art which can explode, diamontinely, in this forever time, in the integrity of the Book—to play them, but and by a triumphant reversal, with the tacit injunction that nothing, pulsing in the unknown womb of the hour, shown in the pages as clear and evident, is to find this readily or perhaps another which this may illuminate.

MARY ANN CAWS

THE BOOK: A SPIRITUAL INSTRUMENT

I am the author of a statement to which there have been varying reactions, including praise and blame, and which I shall make again in the present article. Briefly, it is this: all earthly existence must ultimately be contained in a book.

It terrifies me to think of the qualities (among them genius, certainly) which the author of such a work will have to possess. I am one of the unpossessed. We will let that pass and imagine that it bears no author's name. What, then, will the work itself be? I answer: a hymn, all harmony and joy; an immaculate grouping of universal relationships come together for some miraculous and glittering occasion. Man's duty is to observe with the eyes of the divinity; for if his connection with that divinity is to be made clear, it can be expressed only by the pages of the open book in front of him.

Seated on a garden bench where a recent book is lying, I like to watch a passing gust half open it and breathe life into many of its outer aspects, which are so obvious that no one in the history of literature has ever thought about them. I shall have the chance to do so now, if I can get rid of my overpowering newspaper. I push it aside; it flies about and lands near some roses as if to hush their proud and feverish whispering; finally, it unfolds around them. I will leave it there along with the silent whispering of the flowers. I formally propose now to examine the differences between this rag and the book, which is supreme. The newspaper is the sea; literature flows into it at will.

Now then—

The foldings of a book, in comparison with the large-sized, open newspaper, have an almost religious significance. But an even greater significance lies in their thickness when they are piled together; for then they form a tomb in miniature for our souls.

Every discovery made by printers has hitherto been absorbed in the most elementary fashion by the newspaper, and can be summed up in the word: Press. The result has been simply a plain sheet of paper upon which a flow of words is printed in the most unrefined manner. The immediacy of this system (which preceded the production of books) has undeniable advantages for the writer; with its endless line of posters and proof sheets it makes for improvisation. We have, in other words, a "daily paper." But who, then, can make the gradual discovery of the meaning of this format, or even of a sort of popular fairyland charm about it? Then again, the leader, which is the most important part, makes its great free way through a thousand obstacles and finally reaches a state of disinterestedness. But what is the result of this victory? It overthrows the advertisement (which is Original Slavery) and, as if it were itself the powered printing press, drives it far back beyond intervening articles onto the fourth page and leaves it there in a mass of incoherent and inarticulate cries. A noble spectacle, without question. After this, what else can the newspaper possibly need in order to overthrow the *book* (even though at the bottom—or rather at its foundation, i.e., the *feuilleton*—it resembles the other in its pagination, thus generally regulating the columns)? It will need nothing, in fact; or practically nothing, if the book delays as it is now doing and carelessly continues to be a drain for it. And since even the book's format is useless, of what avail is that extraordinary addition of foldings (like wings in repose, ready to fly forth again) which constitute its rhythm and the chief reason for the secret contained in its pages? Of what avail the priceless silence living there, and evocative symbols following in its wake, to delight the mind which literature has totally delivered?

Yes, were it not for the folding of the paper and the depths thereby established, that darkness scattered about in the form of black characters could not rise and issue forth in gleams of mystery from the page to which we are about to turn.

The newspaper with its full sheet on display makes improper use of printing—that is, it makes good packing paper. Of course, the obvious and vulgar advantage of it, as everybody knows, lies in its mass production and circulation. But that advantage is secondary to a miracle, in the highest sense of the word: words led back to their origin, which is the twenty-six letters of the alphabet, so gifted with infinity that they will finally consecrate Language. Everything is caught up in their endless variations and then rises out of them in the form of the Principle. Thus typography becomes a rite.

The book, which is a total expansion of the letter, must find its mobility in the letter; and in its spaciousness must establish some nameless system of relationships which will embrace and strengthen fiction.

There is nothing fortuitous in all this, even though ideas may seem to be the slaves of chance. The system guarantees them. Therefore we must pay no attention to the book industry with its materialistic considerations. The making of a book, with respect to its flowering totality, begins with the first sentence. From time immemorial the poet has knowingly placed his verse in the sonnet which he writes upon our minds or upon pure space. We, in turn, will misunderstand the true meaning of this book and the miracle inherent in its structure, if we do not knowingly imagine that a given motif has been properly placed at a certain height on the page, according to its own or to the book's distribution of light. Let us have no more of those successive, incessant, back and forth motions of our eyes, traveling from one line to the next and beginning all over again. Otherwise we will miss that ecstasy in which we become immortal for a brief hour, free of all reality, and raise our obsessions to the level of creation. If we do not actively create in this way (as we would music on the keyboard, turning the pages of a score), we would do better to shut our eyes and dream. I am not asking for any servile obedience. For, on the contrary, each of us has within him that lightning-like initiative which can link the scattered notes together.

Thus, in reading, a lonely, quiet concert is given for our minds, and they in turn, less noisily, reach its meaning. All our mental faculties will be present in this symphonic exaltation; but, unlike music, they will be rarefied, for they partake of thought. Poetry, accompanied by the Idea, is perfect Music, and cannot be anything else.

Now, returning to the case at hand and to the question of books which are read in the ordinary way, I raise my knife in protest, like the cook chopping off chickens' heads.

The virginal foldings of the book are unfortunately exposed to the kind of sacrifice which caused the crimson-edged tomes of ancient times to bleed. I mean that they invite the paper-knife, which stakes out claims to possession of the book. Yet our consciousness alone gives us a far more intimate possession than such a barbarian symbol; for it joins the book now here, now there, varies its melodies, guesses its riddles, and even re-creates it unaided. The folds will have a mark which remains intact and invites us to open or close the pages according to the author's desires. There can be only blindness and discourtesy in so murderous and self-destructive an attempt to destroy the fragile, inviolable book. The newspaper holds the advantage here, for it is not exposed to such treatment. But it is nonetheless an annoying influence; for upon the book—upon the divine and intricate organism required by literature—it inflicts the monotonousness of its eternally unbearable columns, which are merely strung down the pages by hundreds.

"But,"

I hear some one say, "how can this situation be changed?" I shall take space here to answer this question in detail; for the work of art—which is unique or should be—must provide illustrations. A tremendous burst of greatness, of thought, or of emotion, contained in a sentence printed in large type, with one gradually descending line to a page, should keep the reader breathless throughout the book and summon forth his powers of excitement. Around this would be smaller groups of secondary importance, commenting on the main sentence or derived from it, like a scattering of ornaments.

It will be said, I suppose, that I am attempting to flabbergast the mob with a lofty statement. That is true. But several of my close friends must have noticed that there are connections between this and their own instinct for arranging their writings in an unusual and ornamental fashion, halfway between verse and prose. Shall I be explicit? All right, then, just to maintain that reputation for clarity so avidly pursued by our make-everything-clear-and-easy era. Let us suppose that a given writer reveals one of his ideas in theoretical fashion and, quite possibly, in useless fashion, since he is ahead of his time. He well knows that such revelations, touching as they do on literature, should be brought out in the open. And yet he hesitates to divulge too brusquely things which do not yet exist; and thus, in his modesty, and to the mob's amazement, he veils them over.

It is because of those daydreams we have before we resume our reading in a garden that our attention strays to a white butterfly flitting here and there, then disappearing; but also leaving behind it the same slight touch of sharpness and frankness with which I have presented these ideas, and flying incessantly back and forth before the people, who stand amazed.

BRADFORD COOK

Letters (1866-1871)

Never in all my life have I worked so hard as this summer; in fact, I have worked *for* all my life. I have laid the foundations for a magnificent work. Every man has his own special secret. Many men die without having discovered it, and they will not discover it because, when they are dead, neither they nor their secret will remain. I died, and I have risen from the dead with the key to the jewelled treasure of my last spiritual casket. Now I shall open it far from all borrowed inspiration, and its mystery will spread through the most beautiful of heavens. For twenty years I shall take monastic refuge in myself, shunning all publicity, except for private readings with my friends. I am working on everything at once; I mean that everything is so well ordered in me that each sensation is transformed at birth and simply pigeon-holed in a given book or poem. When a poem is ripe, it will fall. You can see that I am imitating the natural law.

I haven't had a moment to explain the enigma of my last letter, and I certainly don't want to *be* an enigma to such good friends as you, even though I sometimes use that way of making other people think about me. . . .

I meant simply that I had just finished planning my entire Work; that I had found the key to myself, the crown, or the center (if you prefer to call it that, so we won't get our metaphors mixed)—the center of myself where, like a sacred spider, I hang on the main threads which I have already spun from my mind. With these—*and at their intersections*—I shall make the miraculous laces which I foresee and which already exist in Beauty's bosom.

I meant that I shall need twenty years for the five volumes of this Work; that I shall be patient and read parts of it to friends like you, and I shall scorn fame as I would any other stupid, worn-out idea. For what is relative immortality—especially since we are often immortal in the minds of idiots—compared to the joy of looking on Eternity and enjoying It within ourselves while we are still alive?

To Villiers de l'Isle-Adam, September 24, 1866

I was dumbfounded by your letter because I really *wanted* to be forgotten; I had intended to be alone in hours of remembrance which even the *Past* itself could not have visited. As for the Future, at least the immediate future, my soul has been destroyed. My thought has gone the limit and thought itself through; it has lost the power to evoke the emptiness spread through its pores and turn it to a matchless Nothingness. Beneath a wave of sensitiveness, I was able to understand the intimate relationship of Poetry to the Universe; and, to make Poetry pure, my design was to divorce It from Dreams and Chance and link It to the idea of that Universe. But, unfortunately, since my soul is made for poetic ecstasy alone, I had no Mind at my disposal (as you have) to clear the way for this idea. And so you will be terrified to hear that I discovered the Idea of the Universe through sensation alone—and that, in order to perpetuate the indelible idea of pure Nothingness, I had to fill my brain with the sensation of absolute Emptiness. The mirror in which the image of Being appeared to me was most often Horror, and you can well imagine how cruelly I am atoning for the precious diamond-light I stole from those indescribable Nights. But I am left with the perfect definition and inward dream of two books, original and yet eternal: one of them a perfect absolute called "Beauty"; the other a personal work called "Sumptuous Allegories of Nothingness." And yet the irony and Tantalian torture is that, if my body is to rise from the dead, I must remain powerless to write them for a long time. For I am in the last stage of nervous exhaustion; my mind is so evilly, so perfectly afflicted that I am often unable to understand even the most banal conversation. And so even this simple, awkward letter I am trying to write you is a dangerous undertaking for me.

Really, I am afraid that I may be *starting* my life with the madness which was the *end* of the great and pitiful Baudelaire—despite the fact that *Eternity* has glittered undeniably in my mind and destroyed whatever sense of Time I may have had.

These last months have been terrifying. My Thought has thought itself through and reached a Pure Idea. What the rest of me has suffered during that long agony, is indescribable. But, fortunately, I am quite dead now, and Eternity Itself is the least pure of all the regions where my Mind can wander—that Mind which is the abiding hermit of its own purity and untouched now even by the reflection of Time. Unfortunately, it was my horrifying sensitivity that brought me to this extremity, and I must veil it over now with outward indifference. That is the only way to recover my lost energy. I achieved a supreme synthesis, and now I am slowly recovering my strength. As you can see, amusement is impossible. And yet how infinitely more impossible it was a few months ago when I struggled with that creature of ancient and evil plumage—God—whom I fortunately defeated and threw to earth. But I had waged that battle on His boney wing, and in a final burst of agony greater than I should have expected from Him, He bore me off again among the Shadows; then victoriously, ecstatically, infinitely, I floated downward until finally one day I looked again in my Venetian mirror and saw the person I had been several months before—the person I had forgotten. I should add—and you must say nothing of this—that the price of my victory is so high that I still need to see myself in this mirror in order to think; and that if it were not in front of me here on the table as I write you, I would become Nothingness again. Which means that I am impersonal now: not the Stéphane you once knew, but one of the ways the Spiritual Universe has found to see Itself, unfold Itself through what used to be me.

So evanescent is my ghostly presence here on earth, that my metamorphoses must be limited to an absolute minimum; otherwise the Universe cannot find Itself in me. Therefore, at this moment of Synthesis, I have outlined the work which is going to be their image: three verse poems, with *Hérodiade* as the overture—poems of a purity which man has never reached and will never reach, perhaps, because I may be simply

the victim of an illusion and the human mind may not be perfect enough
to convert such ideals to reality. Then I will do four prose-poems on the
spiritual idea of Nothingness. I need ten years for all this. Will I live
that long?

And now about you. I think your titles and ideas for poems are mar-
velous. I've gone deeply enough into Nothingness to be able to speak
with authority on the subject. The only reality is Beauty and Its only
perfect expression is Poetry. All the rest is a lie—except for those who
live by the body, by love, or by the mental love that friendship is.
. . . Since you are lucky enough to have a love outside of Poetry, then
love: doubtless in *you,* Being and Idea will find that paradise which
wretched mortals, ignorant and lazy as they are, can only hope to find
in death. Then when you think of the nothingness to come, this twin
happiness you have found will comfort you, and you will think it all
quite natural. As for me, Poetry takes the place of love because it is
enamored of itself, and because this self-lust has a delightful dying fall
in my soul. But I confess that the Knowledge I have acquired (or redis-
covered in the depths of the man I was) would seem insufficient to me—
that my entrance into the last Abyss would be a truly crushing blow—if
I were not able to finish my work; I mean *the Work,* the "Great Work,"
as our ancestors the alchemists used to call it.

To Eugène Lefébure, May 17, 1867

My work was created only by *elimination,* and each newly acquired truth
was born only at the expense of an impression which flamed up and
then burned itself out, so that its particular darkness could be isolated
and I could venture ever more deeply into the sensation of Darkness
Absolute. Destruction was my Beatrice. I can speak of this now because
yesterday I completed the first sketch of my work. It is perfectly out-
lined; it will be imperishable if *I* don't perish. I looked upon it without
ecstasy or fear; I closed my eyes and *saw that it existed.*

But I am not proud of this, my dear fellow; in fact, I am rather sad.
For I have not made these discoveries through the normal development
of my faculties, but through the sinful, hasty, satanic, *easy* way of self-
destruction which, in turn, produced not strength but the sensitiveness

that was destined to lead me to this extreme. I can claim no personal merit in this; on the contrary, it is the fear of remorse (because, impatiently, I disobeyed the natural law) that makes me take refuge in the impersonal, as though indulging in a kind of self-vindication.

The most important thing for me is to live with the utmost care so as to prevent the sickness which, if it comes, will inevitably start in my chest. Up to now, school and lack of sunlight have been very bad for me; I need continual heat. Sometimes I feel like going to Africa and begging! When my work is completed, death won't matter; on the contrary, I shall *need* that rest! Now I must stop, because when my soul is exhausted, I begin to complain about my body or about society, and that is sickening.

I think the healthy thing for man—for reflective nature—is to think with his whole body; then you get a full harmonious thought, like violin strings vibrating in unison with the hollow wooden box. But I think that when thoughts come from the brain alone (the brain I abused so much last summer and part of last winter), they are like tunes played on the squeaky part of the first string—which isn't much comfort for the box; they come and go without ever being *created,* without leaving any trace. For example, I can't recall a single one of those sudden *ideas* I had last year. On Easter day I got a terrible headache from thinking only with my brain, after I had gotten it going with coffee; because it can't get going by itself, and my nerves were probably too tired to respond to any outside impression; I tried to stop thinking that way, and with a tremendous effort I braced the nerves in my chest so as to produce a vibration—still holding on to the thought I was then working on, which became the subject of the vibration, that is, an impression; and so that is the way I am beginning a poem I have been dreaming about for a long time. Ever since then, whenever the crucial hour of synthesis approaches, I say to myself: "I am going to work with my heart"; and then I feel my heart (at those times my whole life is undoubtedly centered in it), and the rest of my body is forgotten, except for the hand that is writing and the living heart, and my poem is begun—*begins itself.* Really, I am shattered. To think I have to go through all that to have a unified vision of the Universe. But if you don't do that, then the only unity you feel is your own existence.

I *had* to stop. My brain was stifled by its Dream and had stopped functioning for lack of any other interest. It would have perished in the midst of its own permanent insomnia. I called upon great Night, Who heard my prayer and spread Her darkness over me. So ended the first phase of my life. Now my consciousness has wearied of the shadows and slowly reawakened. It has fashioned a new man; and when he has been born, he will come again upon his Dream.

In these critical hours, I get glimpses of what my dream has been for these last four years. How near I came to losing it! But now I think I really have it.

But I can't begin working it out right away. First of all, I have to develop the necessary ability and my vision must be ripened, unalterable, and instinctive—as if it had been born long ago and not just yesterday.

Even if I am successful, I'll have to face the fact that it isn't easy to get the general public to accept a work like this. But, after all, it's probably just as well for politics to get along without Literature and decide its fate with guns. That puts Literature on its own.

BRADFORD COOK

Igitur

*This Story is addressed to the Intelligence of the
reader which stages things itself.*

—*S.M.*

OLD STUDY

When the breath of his ancestors wants to blow out the
candle (thanks to which, perhaps, the characters con-
tinue to exist in the book of spells)—he says "Not yet!"

At last he himself, when the noises are silenced, will
forecast something great (no stars? chance annulled?)
from this simple fact that he can bring about shadow by
blowing on the light—

Then, since he will have spoken according to the abso-
lute—which denies immortality, the absolute will exist
outside—moon, above time: and he will raise the curtains
opposite.

Igitur, a very young child, reads his assignment to his
ancestors.

4 PIECES

1. Midnight
2. The Stairs
3. The Dice Throw
4. Sleep on the Ashes, after the Candle is Snuffed Out.

More or less what follows:

Midnight sounds—the Midnight when the dice must be
cast. Igitur descends the stairs of the human mind, goes
to the depths of things: as the "absolute" that he is.
Tombs—ashes (not feeling, nor mind) dead center. He

recites the prediction and makes the gesture. Indiffer-
ence. Hissings on the stairs. "You are wrong": no emo-
tion. The infinite emerges from chance, which you have
denied. You mathematicians expired—I am projected
absolute. I was to finish an Infinite. Simply word and
gesture. As for what I am telling you, in order to explain
my life. Nothing will remain of you—The infinite at last
escapes the family, which has suffered from it—old
space—no chance. The family was right to deny it—its
life—so that it stayed the absolute. This was to take place
in the combinations of the Infinite face to face with the
Absolute. Necessary—the extracted Idea. Profitable mad-
ness. There one of the acts of the universe was just
committed. Nothing else, the breath remained, the end
of word and gesture united—blow out the candle of
being, by which all has been. Proof.

(Think on that)

I

MIDNIGHT

Certainly a presence of Midnight subsists. The hour
did not disappear through a mirror, did not bury itself
in curtains, evoking a furnishing by its vacant sonority.
I remember that its gold was going to feign in its ab-
sence a null jewel of reverie, rich and useless survival,
except that upon the marine and stellar complexity of a
worked gold the infinite chance of conjunctions was
to be read.

A revealer of midnight, it had never yet indicated such
a conjuncture, for here is the single hour it had created;
and so from the Infinite constellations and the sea are
separated, remaining reciprocal nothingness on the out-
side, to permit its essence, united to the hour, to form
the absolute present of things.

And the presence of Midnight remains in the vision
of a room of time where the mysterious furnishing ar-

rests a vague quiver of thought, a luminous break of the return of its waves and their first expansion, while (within a moving limit) the former place of the hour's fall is immobilized in a narcotic calm of the pure *self* long dreamed-of; but whose time is resolved in draperies upon which is arrested the quivering now subsided, adding its splendor to those draperies in a forgetfulness, like hair languishing about the host's face, lit with mystery, with eyes null like the mirror, stripped of any meaning other than presence.

It is the pure dream of a Midnight disappeared into itself, whose Brightness recognized and alone remaining in the center of its accomplishment plunged into the shadow, sums up its sterility on the pallor of an open book presented by the table; ordinary page and setting of the Night except that the silence of an antique utterance it proffered still subsists, in which this returned Midnight evokes its shadow, finite and null, with these words: I was the hour which is to make me pure.

Long since dead, a dead idea contemplates itself as idea by the brightness of the chimera in which its dream agonized, and recognizes itself in the immemorial vacant gesture with which it invites itself, in order to finish the antagonism of this polar dream, with both a chimerical clarity and the re-closed text, to go toward the miscarried Chaos of the dark and the utterance which absolved Midnight, and surrender to them.

Useless, from the accomplished furnishing which will pile up in the darkness like draperies, already made heavy in a permanent form while in a virtual glimmer, produced by its own apparition in the mirroring of obscurity, the pure fire of the clock diamond glitters, the sole survivor and jewel of eternal Night: the hour is formulated in this echo, at the threshold of the panels opened by its act of Night: "Farewell, night that I was, your own sepulchre, but which, the shadow surviving, will metamorphose into Eternity."

II

HE LEAVES THE ROOM AND IS LOST ON THE STAIRS

(instead of sliding down the banister)

The shadow having disappeared into obscurity, Night remained with a dubious perception of a pendulum about to be extinguished and expire there; but by whatever gleams and is about to be extinguished and expire, night sees itself bearing the pendulum; doubtless it was thus the source of the detected beating, whose sounds, complete and ever bare, fell into its past.

If on one hand the ambiguity ceased, on the other a motion persists, marked as more pressing by a double blow which no longer attains its notion or not yet, and whose present brushing, such as must have taken place, confusingly fills the ambiguity or its cessation: as if the complete fall, which the single shock of the tomb doors has been, did not stifle the guest irremediably; and in the uncertainty the affirmative cast probably caused, prolonged by the reminiscence of the sepulchral emptiness of the blow in which clarity is confused, comes a vision of the interrupted fall of the panels, as if it were one who, endowed with the suspended motion, turned it back on itself in the resulting dizzy spiral; and the spiral would have escaped indefinitely if some progressive oppression—a gradual weight of what was not realized although it had on the whole been explicated—had not implied the certain escape in an interval, the cessation; when at the moment the blow expired and oppression and escape were mixed, nothing was heard further: except for the beating of absurd wings of some terrified denizen of the night, startled in his heavy slumber by the brightness, and prolonging his indefinite flight.

For, the gasping which had grazed this place was not some last doubt of the self, which by chance stirred its wings in passing, but the familiar and continual friction of a superior age, of which many a genius was careful to gather all the secular dust into his sepulchre in order to look into a clean self, and so that no suspicion might climb back up the spidery thread—so that the last shadow might look into its proper self and recognize itself in the crowd of its apparitions understood by the nacreous star of their nebulous science held in one hand and by the golden sparkle of the heraldic clasp of their volume held in the other; the volume of their nights; such at present, seeing themselves so that it might see itself, the Shadow, pure and having its last form that it treads on left lying down behind, and then before it in a well, the stretch of layers of shadow, returned to pure night, of all its similar nights, its layers forever separated from them and which they probably did not recognize—which is no other, I know, than the absurd prolongation of the sound of the sepulchral door closing, of which the entrance to this well is reminiscent.

This time, no more doubt; certainty is reflected in the evidence: in vain, the memory of a lie whose consequence was itself, did the vision of a place appear again, such for example as the awaited interval was to be, having in fact for lateral walls the double opposition of the panels, and for the front and back, the opening of a void doubt echoed by the prolongation of the noise of the panels, where the plumage took flight, and doubled by the ambiguity explored, the perfect symmetry of the foreseen deductions denied its reality; no possible mistaking, it was the consciousness of self (for which even the absurd itself was to serve as a place)—succeeding.

It is present equally in one and the other surface of the shining and secular walls, retaining only in one hand the opal brightness of its knowledge, and in the other, its volume, the volume of its nights, now closed, of the past and the future which the pure shadow, having attained the pinnacle of myself, perfectly dominates, and finished, outside themselves. While before and behind is prolonged the explored lie of the infinite, the darkness of all my apparitions gathered together now that time has ceased and divides them no longer, fallen back into a massive, heavy slumber (at the time of the sound first heard), in the void of which I hear the pulsations of my own heart.

I do not like this sound: this perfection of my certainty bothers me; all is too clear, the clarity reveals a desire to escape. Everything gleams too brightly; I should like to return to my anterior uncreated Shadow, and through thought to rid myself of the disguise which necessity has imposed upon me, inhabiting the heart of this race (which I hear beating here) the sole remains of ambiguity.

In truth, in this disturbing and beautiful symmetry of my dream's construction, which of the two openings to take, because the future is represented no longer by one of them? Are they not both forever equivalent, my reflection? Must I still fear chance, that antique enemy which divided me into darkness and created time, both pacified there in the same slumber? and is it not itself annulled by the end of time, which brought about that of darkness?

(whispering)

Indeed, the first spiral to come reflects the preceding one: the same rhythmical sound—and the same brushing; but since everything has ended, nothing can any longer frighten me; my fright which had made the first move in the form of a bird is far distant: has it not been replaced by the apparition of what I had been? and which I like to reflect now, in order to disengage my dream from that costume?

Was not this scansion the sound of the progress of my character which now continues it in the spiral, and this brushing the brushing of its duality? Finally, it is not the hairy stomach of some inferior guest within me, whose doubt the light struck and who fled with a flutter, but the velvet bust of an anterior race the light annoyed and who breathes in a stifling air, of a character whose thought has no consciousness of itself, of my last figure, separated from its person by a spider's ruff and who does not know itself; so, now that his duality is forever separated and I do not even hear any longer through him the sound of his progress, I shall forget myself through him, and dissolve myself in me.

Its impact becomes unsteady once more as it did before having had the perception of itself: it was the scansion of my measure whose memory came back to me prolonged both by the sound in the temporal corridor of the door to my sepulchre, and by hallucination: and just as it was really closed, even so it must open now for my dream to have been explained to itself.

The hour of my leaving has sounded, the purity of the mirror will be established, without this character, a vision of myself—but he will take away the light!—the night! Over the vacant furniture, the Dream has agonized in this glass flask, purity which encloses the substance of Nothingness.

He leaves the room

III
IGITUR'S LIFE
(*Schema*)

Listen, my race, before snuffing out my candle—to the account of my life I have to render you—Here: neurosis, boredom (or Absolute!).

I have always lived with my soul fixed upon the clock. Indeed, I have tried for the time it sounded to *remain* present in the room, its becoming for me both nourishment and life—I made the curtains thicker, and as I was obliged to be seated across from this mirror, in order not to doubt myself, I gathered up preciously the least atoms of time in cloths ceaselessly made thicker.—The clock has often done me a great deal of good.

Empty hours, purely negative

(That before his Idea had been completed? *Indeed, Igitur was projected out of time by his race.*)

Here in sum is Igitur, since his Idea has been completed: —The understood past of his race weighing on him in the feeling of the finite, the hour of the clock precipitating this boredom in a heavy and stifling time, and his expectation of future accomplishment, all form pure time, or boredom, rendered unstable by the malady of ideality: this boredom, not able to be, becomes, as in the beginning, its elements once more, all the furniture closed up and full of its secret; and Igitur, as if menaced by the torture of being eternal of which he has a vague foretaste, seeking himself in the mirror become boredom, and seeing himself vague and about to disappear as if he were going to fade away into time, then evoking himself; then at the moment when he has recovered from all this boredom of time, seeing the mirror horribly null, seeing himself there surrounded by a rarefaction, an absence of atmosphere, and the furniture twisting its chimeras in the void, and the curtains invisibly trembling, uneasy; then, he opens the furniture to free its mystery, the unknown, its memory, its silence, human faculties and impressions—and when he believes he has become himself once more, his soul fixedly contemplates the clock, whose hour disappears through the mirror spilling over it or goes to burrow in the curtains, overflowing, not even leaving him to the boredom he implores and dreams of. Impotent even of boredom.

He separates from time indefinite, and he is! And this time will not stop, as formerly, with a grey shiver on the massive ebonies whose chimeras closed their lips with a wearying feeling of the finite, and no longer mixing with the saturated and weighted draperies, will not fill a mirror with boredom, where suffocating and stifled, I begged a vague figure disappearing completely, fused with the glass, to remain; until finally, when my hands were removed an instant from my eyes where I had placed them so as not to see it disappear in a frightful sensation of eternity in which the room seemed to expire, it appeared to me like the horror of that eternity. And when I opened my eyes in the depths of this mirror, I saw the character of horror, the phantom of horror absorb little by little what remained in the mirror of feeling and pain, nourishing his horror with the supreme shivers of chimeras and the instability of the draperies, and form himself making the mirror rarer until it reached an unbelievable purity—until he was detached, permanent, from the mirror absolutely pure, as if frozen—until at last the furniture, its monsters having succumbed with their convulsive rings, lay dead in a severe and isolated posture, projecting their hard lines in an absence of atmosphere, the monsters rigid in their last struggle, and the curtains fell, their unrest quieted, in a position they were to hold forever.

IV
THE DICE THROW
IN THE TOMB
(*Schema*)

Briefly, in an act where chance is in play, chance always accomplishes its own Idea in affirming or negating itself. Confronting its existence, negation and affirmation fail. It contains the Absurd—implies it, but in the latent state and prevents it from existing: which permits the Infinite to be.

The Dice Horn is the unicorn's Horn—the one-horned.

But the Act accomplishes itself.

Then his self is manifested in his reassuming Madness, admitting the act, and voluntarily reassuming the Idea as Idea, and the Act (whatever the power that guided it) having denied chance, he concludes from it that the Idea has been necessary.

—Then he conceives that there is, to be sure, madness in admitting it absolutely: but at the same time he can say that since through this madness, chance was denied, this madness was necessary. For what? (No one knows that he is isolated from humanity.)

All there is to it is that his race has been pure: that it took from the Absolute its purity to be so, and to leave of it only an Idea itself ending up in Necessity; and that as for the Act, it is perfectly absurd except as movement (personal) returned to the Infinite: but that the Infinite is at last *fixed*.

Igitur simply shakes the dice—a motion, before going to rejoin the ashes, the atoms of his ancestors: the movement, which is in him, is absolved. It is understood what its ambiguity means.

He closes the book—snuffs out the candle—with his breath which contained chance: and, folding his arms, lies down on the ashes of his ancestors.

Folding his arms—the Absolute has disappeared, in the purity of his race (for that is necessary, because the sound ceases).

Immemorial race, whose burdensome time has fallen, excessive, into the past, and which race, full of chance, has lived, then, only on its future.—This chance denied with the aid of an anachronism, a character as a supreme incarnation of this race—who feels in himself, thanks to the absurd, the existence of the Absolute, has only forgotten human speech within the book of spells, and the thought in a luminary one announcing this negation of chance, the other clarifying the dream where it has arrived. The character who, believing in the existence of the sole Absolute, imagines he is everywhere in a dream (he acts from the Absolute point of view), finds the act useless, for there is and is not chance—he reduces chance to the *Infinite*—which, he says, must exist somewhere.

A throw of the dice which accomplishes a prediction, on which depended the life of a race. "Don't hiss," to the winds, to the shadows —If I plan, as an actor, to play the trick—the 12—no chance in any sense.

He proffers the prediction, about which he secretly does not care. There has been madness.

V

HE LIES DOWN IN THE TOMB

Upon the ashes of stars, the undivided ones of the
family, lay the poor character, after having drunk the   *or the dice—*
drop of nothingness lacking to the sea. (The empty   *chance ab-*
flask, madness, all that remains of the castle?) Nothing-   *sorbed*
ness having departed, there remains the castle of purity.

MARY ANN CAWS

TWO NOTES ON *IGITUR*

With Hamlet there appeared a theme . . . which waited two centuries
to find an atmosphere it could develop in: the attraction to Night, the
penchant for unhappiness, the bitter communion between the shadows
and this anguish of being mortal.

. . . Lamp, mirror, dresser, curtains, clock, library, dice: the whole
stifling and stuffy furniture of the Victorian era . . . where a new
kind of dreamer, with a cigar between his fingers, takes the place of
the one in "The Raven." Outside, only despairing darkness . . . It is
remarkable that the fate of this prince of a modern Elsinore should end
in his taking up and developing once more Igitur's supreme gesture,
this roll of dice into the night, not unlike Pascal's wager, this haughty
splendor of a great lord throwing down his purse, this abdication of a
wise man awaiting nothing else from science or from art (in short,
from numbers), this recognition that the contingent will never be able
to form the absolute or to produce anything other than a combination
precarious and as such, useless.

PAUL CLAUDEL, "The Catastrophe of *Igitur*"
(*Nouvelle revue française,* Nov. 1, 1926)

MARY ANN CAWS

Igitur is Mallarmé's vision of an implacably daring and stubborn explorer of the unknown like himself, with echoes of Hamlet and of an immemorial occult tradition of initiation into life's rock-bottom mysteries, going back to ancient lore like the Upanishads, the Greek and early Christian mystics, and the Hebrew Kabbalah and rising in time to modern figures like Swedenborg, Böhme, Poe, Balzac, Nerval. In sum, this is the spiritual adventure described by, among others, Carl Jung in *Psyche and Symbol* and Joseph Campbell in his *Hero with a Thousand Faces;* a descent into the dark womb of the unconscious, eternal night, and reemergence, rebirth to a vision of undying light and truth. The hero strips himself of earthly clutter, becomes as naked as a babe. It is a sacrificial, bitter experience, involving a psychic suicide, a baptismal plunge into unbreathable depths of the self and the cosmos.

For this initiatory moment, at a dark Midnight in a claustral room with drawn curtains where space as well as time is annulled to a mere diamond-point of ultimate consciousness, the solitary spirit communes with his dead ancestors who have handed him down a mysterious mandate in a magic book, illuminated by a single candle which at the fateful instant he will blow out, leaving only a deathly blackness and void. Then the hero will throw the dice of universal chance, accepting its absurdity as he does death-anguish, in order to find true Meaning and Life.

ROBERT GREER COHN, *Mallarmé's Igitur*
(*University of California Press, 1981*)

Un Coup de dés jamais
n'abolira le hasard/Dice Thrown
Never Will Annul Chance

PREFACE

I'd choose for this Note not to be read, or then for it to be forgotten once glanced at; it has little to teach that goes beyond any skillful Reader's own penetration, and may bother the naïve reader who has to look at the first words of the Poem so that the following ones—spread out as they are—lead on to the last ones with nothing new except a certain distribution of space made within the reading. The "blanks" in fact assume an importance, striking first: versification required them like a surrounding silence, to such an extent that a lyric piece or one with a few feet usually takes up about a third of the leaf on which it is centered: I don't transgress against this system, but simply disperse it. The paper intervenes every time an image on its own, ceases or retires within the page, accepting the succession of the others, and it is not a question, unlike the usual state of affairs, of regular sound effects or verses—rather of prismatic subdivisions of the idea, the instant when they appear and during which their cooperation lasts, in some exact mental setting. The text imposes itself in various places, near or far from the latent guiding thread, according to what seems to be the probable sense.

The literary advantage, if I may put it like that, of this copied distance which mentally separates groups of words or words between themselves, seems to be now to speed along and now again to slow down the motion, scanning it, even intimating it according to some simultaneous vision of the Page, the latter taken as a unit as in the verse or the perfect line elsewhere. The fiction will come to the surface and rapidly dissipate as the writing shifts about, around the fragmentary halts of the sentence, predominant from the time the title is introduced through its continuation. Everything happens by a shortcut, hypothetically; storytelling is avoided. Add to that: that from this naked use of thought, retreating, prolonging, fleeing, or from its very design, there results for the person reading it aloud, a musical score. The difference in the printed characters between the preponderant, secondary, and adjacent motifs, dictates their importance for oral expression; the disposition of the characters: in the middle, on the top, or the bottom of the page, indicates the rise and fall in intonation. In my work, which has no precedent, there remain only a few daring rubrics, turns, and so on forming the counterpoint of prosody in the elementary state; not that I deem the opportunity of essays timid; but it does not behoove me outside of my own special pages or volume, even in a courageous Review, however generous and open to freedom it shows itself to be, to act in a fashion too contrary to custom. All the same, I will have indicated about this Poem, more than the sketch, a "state" which does not at all break with tradition, adjusting its presentation so as not to offend anyone, just enough to open some eyes. Today, or at least without presuming anything about the future which will follow from this, nothing or almost an art, let us openly acknowledge that the attempt shares, unexpectedly, in the particular pursuits dear to our time, free verse and the prose poem. Their meeting takes place under an influence I know to be odd, that of Music as it is heard at a concert. Quite a few techniques found therein seem to me to belong to Letters, and so I pick them up. Let the genre become one like the symphony, little by little, beside the personal declamation, leaving ancient verse intact—I venerate it and attribute to it the empire of passion and of dream—while it would be the time to treat, preferably, as it follows naturally, subjects of pure and complex imagination or intellect, not to exclude them from Poetry—the unique source.

—STÉPHANE MALLARMÉ
(*translated by Mary Ann Caws*)

DICE THROWN

NEVER

WHEN EVEN INDEED CAST IN CIRCUMSTANCES

OF ETERNITY

FROM THE DEPTH OF A SHIPWRECK

BE

    that

           the Abyss

   blanched
     slackwater
        raging

                    slanted
              glides despairingly even
                       some wing

                      its own

                          be-

forehand fallen back from incapacity to trim the flight
and covering what foams
cutting back what soars

most inwardly resumes

the shadow buried within the deep by this alternative sail

to the point of fitting
to wing-span

its yawning deep in so far forth as the shell

of a ship

listed to one or th' other board

THE MASTER

risen
inferring

from this conflagration

that there

as one threatens

the unique Number which can not

hesitates
corpse by the arm

rather
than to play
as hoar fanatic
the hand
in the name of the waves

one

shipwreck that

      beyond old-time cypherings
    where the manoeuvre with age forgotten

        once he was wont to grasp the helm

at his feet
      from the unanimous horizon

readies itself
   works itself up and mingles
     with the fist which would grip it
a destiny and the winds

be another

      Spirit
        to hurl it
           to the tempest
             to undo division and to pass on proud

separated from the secret it pens

invades the head
flows as beard subdued below

strict of the man

    barkless
      little it matters
        where vain

ancestrally to not open the hand
                        clenched
                beyond the useless head

        legacy amid vanishment

                for some one
                        ambiguous

                the ulterior immemorial demon
having
        from null lands
                induced
the ancient towards this supreme conjunction with probability

                        he
                        his puerile shade
caressed and polished and rendered and washed
                suppled by the wave and withdrawn
                from the hard bones lost among the timbers

                        born
                        of play
the sea via the old one trying or the old one against the sea
                a useless chance

                                Betrothals

of which
        the illusory veil spun again their hauntingness
        like the ghost of a geste

                        will totter
                        will collapse

                        madness

WILL ANNUL

AS IF

An insinuation

in the silence

in some neighboring

hovers

merely

rolled up in irony
                or
                    the mystery
                            flung down
                                    howled out

whirlpool of hilarity and horror

about the gulf
                    without strewing it
                            nor fleeing

                    and of it cradles the virginal trace

                                                    AS IF

quill solitary desperate

except that

encounters or grazes it a midnight toque
and immobilises
in velvet crumpled by a burst of dark laughter

this stiff white

laughable
opposed to the sky
too much
not to brand
exiguously
whosoever

bitter prince of the reef

dons it like the heroic
irresistible but contained
within his small virile reason
in a flash

under the weather
      scapegoat pubescent

                              mute

                    The lucid and lordly aigrette
                      invisible on the brow
                  glitters
                          then shadows
                      a stature minion darkling
                        in its siren twist

                  with impatient terminal scales

                        laugh

                    that

                IF

of vastness

standing

        the time
                to slap
forked

            a rock

        false manor
                instantly
                    dispersed in mist

                    which laid
                        a limit on infinity

IT WAS
born of stars

IT WOULD BE
    worse

             nor

                    more nor less

                                 indifferently but as much

THE NUMBER
MIGHT IT EXIST

otherwise than hallucination of scattered spray
MIGHT IT BEGIN AND MIGHT IT END

welling up as denied and bounded on show
at last
in some outpouring rarely spread
MIGHT IT BE COUNTED

evidence of a tot of the sum however little one
MIGHT IT ILLUMINE

CHANCE

Drops
the quill
rhythmical suspending of defeat
to bury itself
in the original spray
whence but lately whose frenzy sprang as far as a peak
blasted
by the identical neutrality of the gulf

NOTHING

of the memorable crisis
or might have
the event

come about of itself in view of every result nul
human

WILL HAVE TAKEN PLACE
an everyday uplifting pours out absence

BUT PLACE
commonplace plashing below of waves as for dispersing the empty act
abruptly which otherwise
by its lie
had founded
perdition

in these reaches

of the vague

in which all the real dissolves

EXCEPTED
            at the summit
                    PERHAPS

                            as far as one place

fuses with beyond
                                outside the interest
                     for its part signalled
                                     in general
by such obliquity on such declivity
                                       of fires

       towards
         that should be
            Septentrion also North

                            A CONSTELLATION

              cold of forgetfulness and disuse
                        not so much
                    as to not enumerate
              on some vacant and superior surface
                    the shock successive
                             starwise
             of a total count in the making

waking
       doubting
           rolling
              shining and musing

                     before halting
             at some latest point which crowns it

                All Thought utters Dice Thrown

BRIAN COFFEY

New Directions Paperbooks—A Partial Listing

For complete listing request free catalog from
New Directions, 80 Eighth Avenue, New York 10011

†Bilingu

For complete listing request free catalog from
New Directions, 80 Eighth Avenue, New York 10011